Dedicated to

My students... the ultimate teachers.

Begin the Journey

With an

Open Heart...

The Zen of Singing ©

The Zen of Singing

Freeing Your True Voice

By: Karen Gallinger

The Zen of Singing ©

Introduction

Why *The Zen of Singing*? Because as a singer I discovered the need to become highly conscious, and then release that consciousness, that I also found in Zen, an awareness of the smallest thing and how it affects, even defines, the larger thing. It is also necessary for me to clear my ego and personal baggage so that the muse may move unobstructed through me. For me, singing and performance are a connection to the transcendent. Yet, there is also a nuts and bolts aspect of the craft that needs to be understood and incorporated. There are many books about technique, and there are some books about the spiritual aspects of performance. The challenge for me was trying to find a way to combine these two elements in an understandable way. I hope this book does that.

As a professional singer and a voice teacher I have been on both sides of the vocal experience. There were times when good technique got me through a tough gig, as well as times when the "book learning" aspects of technique just didn't apply. Trial, error, and adjustment were the norm. The subject can be very abstract at times and often depends wholly on the way in which you experience your own body.

This book is the product of many years of discovery, both on the gig and through private study. Some of the concepts may be familiar to you; some of them are a direct result of my personal experience. It is not meant to be the "definitive" singing book, merely another source of information to familiarize you with basic concepts. It is up to you to experiment, apply the information, and do the work necessary to put you on the path to discovering your own voice.

At the end of several of the chapters there is room for you to take notes. You can use the space to do some of the exercises, or just jot down thoughts and questions that may arise as you read. Periodically review what you have written so you can explore it further, perhaps in your journal. Look at things from many different angles, not just the familiar views. Connect the dots in new ways. Play with the ideas... You already have a wealth of information stored away in your head. You will probably be surprised at how you can resolve issues by using what you already know, but shifting your perspective a bit.

While singing is a unique journey for each person, there is much common ground. Especially when it comes to technique and understanding your instrument. The word "technique" sometimes scares singers; especially pop singers, since it is often accompanied by images of Opera singers, hall-filling voices, and Italian or German text. In fact, "technique" is merely the set of tools you have available to you so you can make choices about how you want to sound. What you create with these tools is up to you, but the better the tools and your ability to use them, the better the final result will be. Your goal should be to become the driver, rather than a mere passenger on your vocal journey.

No one can learn to sing well entirely out of a book. You will need some good, knowledgeable feedback as you work, so finding a good teacher is important. Look for a teacher who is flexible about style. There is no use studying with someone who wants to turn you into a version of them. A good teacher will help you discover your own style. Also, if the work they have you doing hurts or causes strain, run for the hills! Finally, find someone you can relate to and who makes you feel comfortable. There is nothing worse than dreading your lessons because you are intimidated by, or afraid of, your teacher. Singing should be fun, not scary!

The Zen of Singing ©

I often tell my students that music is 75% Math, and 25% Magic. Anyone can learn the Math, but you must move beyond just the mathematical or technical aspects of music, or neither you nor the audience ever never quite get to the transcendent experience. Technique will lead you to the door of the Magic; you must approach that door with humility so it will open and welcome you. If you come armed with arrogance, it will remain locked and never reveal itself to you.

How do you open the door to the transcendent experience? First of all, learn the <u>craft</u> of singing. Make sure your technique is solid and the mechanical aspects of the song are firmly in place. Then, give yourself over completely to the music, and... let go.

I once had a teacher say to me "Don't be afraid to show your Fool." I was very young and completely wrapped up in my fear, so at the time it made no sense to me. Don't be afraid to look foolish or make a mistake? What are you, nuts?!? But, over the years I began to embrace the fundamental truth in that statement, and it changed my life.

Fear is a giant brick wall. Most of us are afraid of revealing our Fool to anyone. But, guess what? EVERYONE has one! Imagine you have a little closet locked away where the Fool lives. The Fool is never allowed out because you just never know what he or she is likely to do, and it may embarrass you. OK... Click, locked up tight. Safe.

There are two problems with that solution. First, The Fool is a tricky litter bugger and will manage to sneak out at the most inopportune times, and embarrass you anyway. The second problem is, The Fool is not alone in that closet. Stuck in there behind The Fool is The Creative one. If you don't let The Fool out for air now and then, how will The Creative one ever get out? The Fool is the link to your Creative side, so let them BOTH out to play! The Fool will lead you to your Creativity, so celebrate them both!!

The exercises in this book are a combination of observation, visualization, and vocalizing. Try them all. You may immediately relate to some and not feel comfortable with others. That is fine. Use the exercises that work best for you. Your progress is a very personal thing, and it is directly proportional to the amount of time you spend working toward your goal. If you take lessons, no matter how bright you are a 1/2-hour lesson per week with little or no practice on your own will get you nowhere. So please ... make the commitment to yourself to spend the time and energy necessary to reach your goal.

Speaking of goals, you need to identify clearly what yours are; be realistic. Studying voice is the same as studying any other instrument. Would you expect to begin playing the violin, flute, or piano and become a virtuoso within a few months? Studying voice takes time, work, and patience. Set goals you can reach. Be sure to give yourself credit for progress made, and don't beat yourself up if you don't progress as quickly as you might like! As long as you are truly making the effort you will improve. Trust that and relax into the process. It will make the journey much easier.

The best reason to study singing is for the joy of singing. Anything else that comes out of it, such as recognition or money, is merely icing. While the goal of voice training is to become the master of your craft rather than be at the mercy of your lack of mastery, what I really hope you learn from studying is that singing is an act of love. It is spiritual, it is joyful, it is freeing, and finding your voice, whatever it may be, is one of the greatest gifts you can ever give yourself. It is a journey, complete with ups and downs, missed paths, new roads and much discovery. Welcome!

The Zen of Singing ©

The Zen of Singing

Take a Breath,

Focus,

Begin ...

The Zen of Singing ©

Table of Contents

Each chapter concludes with a section of Tips, Exercises and a page for taking notes.

Sidebars

Illustrations

<u>You</u>

Are

The Instrument...

The Zen of Singing ©

1. Overview

Being a good singer requires technique, talent and hard work.

Technique

The vocal instrument can be broken down into 3 different "parts":

- **Breathing:** The way you support and sustain the tone *(See Chapter 5)*

- **Placement:** The effective use of your resonators and the shape/sound of the tone *(See Chapter 6)*

- **The Larynx:** Your voice box, which actually creates the vibration/sound *(See Chapter 7)*

Each of these 3 parts of the voice must be understood and coordinated individually and then coordinated together as a unit. There are many other things to consider when approaching singing. But until you have a clear concept and control of these things, the progress you can make in other areas will be limited.

I use the whole body approach. Since your body is your instrument, I encourage you to become aware of how your body works and how the act of singing affects your entire body, not just the limited experience that most people have of feeling it in their throat, which, by the way, is exactly where you don't want to feel it. *(More on that later.)*

Musicality

Some people have a great natural gift for music; others struggle to sing in tune. No matter what your level of ability, with work you can improve. Believe it or not, the most important skill you need as a singer is LISTENING! Learning to listen effectively can, all by itself, greatly improve your singing skills.

Familiarize yourself with the basic structure of music: Rhythm, Pitch, and Form. Learn about the patterns and simple formulas that are used to construct music, and you will greatly improve your ability to maneuver your way through a song with ease.

Performance

Not everyone is cut out to be a performer, but everyone should be able to enjoy singing. Whether singing alone, with friends, in the privacy of your own home, in a choir, or in the neighborhood Karaoke bar, singing can be great fun.

While singing is a wonderful form of self-expression, all singing will not, cannot, and should not lead to a professional career. Let your goal be joy, not money. If the money follows, great; if not, you still have the joy.

If you are one of the people blessed with the gifts of a good voice, a musical sensibility, and a desire to perform... learn your craft! A working knowledge of technique, music theory, and performance skills are the bare minimum requirements to do you and those you work with justice.

The Zen of Singing ©

10 Basic Rules of Voice Production

1. RELAX - No tension. This means physically as well as mentally

2. Your body responds to thought, so always think of the voice as floating or being gently lifted. NEVER use images that make you push, shove, or pull the sound.

3. Do not sing FROM the throat. The tone should resonate in the head, mainly the mouth and sinus cavities, and sometimes, sympathetically in the chest. It should NOT be focused in the throat.

4. Attack from your diaphragm, keeping the throat relaxed and open so the sound may pass freely through it. Do not allow tension or involvement of the " Swallowing Muscles."

5. Keep your jaw relaxed. Articulate with your tongue, lips, and teeth.

6. Good posture is important. Stand straight, shoulders rolled back and relaxed; otherwise, proper breathing is obstructed.

7. Keep your tongue relaxed and down.

8. Diaphragmatic breathing is necessary for correct support. Always support. Lack of support brings unnecessary muscles into play, causing strain. Straining can cause damage to your vocal cords. In extreme cases the damage can be permanent!

9. Singing and speaking are both natural functions and are very similar. Allow yourself to sing as naturally as you allow yourself to speak.

10. Remember: singing correctly is easy! If you are pushing, straining, or feeling tension or pain, then you are doing it wrong.

Big Goals,

Little Steps...

The Zen of Singing ©

2. Warming Up and Practice

Practice makes possible...

The Exercise CD that is included with this book is a very basic group of scales, intervals, and arpeggios that will give you a simple warm up. There are many method CD's available with more strenuous vocal workouts for flexibility and range, so as you master the included set of examples, I encourage you to find some that will challenge you further.

Warm up exercises serve two purposes. The first is obviously to warm up your instrument. Think of your voice as a muscle. Before you get into a serious workout for strength and endurance, you want to gently limber up; it gets your body warmed up and ready to perform. Your voice also needs warming up before you put it to any serious use. Approach the warm up exercises as a way to ease into using your instrument.

Second, because the exercises on the CD are very simple, you can memorize them quickly. Then you are free to focus your attention on basic technique, instead of trying to struggle through a series of really tough exercises.

Once you are comfortable with the exercises, start paying attention to how you make the sound. *Close your eyes and focus on the sensations.*

These are just a few questions to ask yourself:

- Where is the sound?
- What does it feel like?
- What does it sound like?

- Is the sound breathy? Consistent? ... What about H's?
- Can you change the quality or placement? How?

The point is to become conscious. Be aware of your instrument and how it works, so you can make choices about how you want to use it. *Choose* the sound that comes out of you. Don't just open your mouth and hope for the best. Experiment, work hard, and be willing to risk.... Take chances! Don't worry about falling down or feeling foolish. Failure is not the lack of immediate success. Failure is not trying.

Singing involves your voice, your ears, and your mind.

YOU MUST TRAIN ALL THREE...

SING... LISTEN ... and THINK!

Be the master of your instrument, not the other way around. Find your own style, and be true to yourself.

Remember, the goal is awareness!

Practice

PAY ATTENTION to what you are doing. Don't just practice mindlessly. It is better to work for 10 focused minutes than 30 mindless minutes. You want to build stamina, but don't push. It's the warm up, not the race. Focus on 3 or 4 exercises per session and include songs in your daily practice. Make it fun! Master your technique in practice, so you can relax and count on it in performance.

You must be clear about the sound you are making. You must also get clear about the sound you want to make. Hear the sound in your head. Don't just make a sound and try to fix it halfway through. You must begin your "focus" before you start the sound and maintain it until it is finished.

The Zen of Singing ©

This is the order in which things must happen:

Intention ~ Action ~ End of action ~ End of intention.

If your focus is not locked in before the action, or if it wavers before the conclusion of the action, the result will be a sloppy tone.

On a Scale of 1-10 ...

Trying to clarify degrees of Volume, Breathiness, or Tone Color can be confusing at first. I find it helps to create a standard. I call it installing the "VU Meter". *(Vocal Understanding)*

Starting with Volume:

Sing and hold the loudest note you can. Designate this as "10". Then sing and hold the very softest note you can. Designate this as "1". Go back and forth between the two until you have a sense of consistency. Now that you have established the extremes, sing a note that would be a "5" on the meter. Practice all three volume levels until you feel comfortable. Then add a "3" and a "7". Continue until you have clarified your Volume Meter. Use the same process for any other aspects you need to break down and clarify.

As you learn to narrow your focus you will learn to control your instrument much more effectively!

Where to practice

If you can create your own personal practice space, that would be wonderful! Preferably somewhere people, noise, or phones will not disturb you. However, many singers don't have that luxury, so you need to make due with what you have. Don't let the lack of a perfect practice room be a deterrent to practicing. *(Yeah.... the bad news is: you have to practice!)*

The shower is not a bad place to practice. The nice warm steam relaxes your instrument, and the tiles tend to resonate well. Bring your CD player in and sing away. Just remember to focus.

The car is not a great place to practice. Besides the fact that you need to concentrate on driving, the ambient noise and the fact that you are sitting make it far less than optimal. Still, for some people it's the only chance they may have. So, if you must, sit straight, don't over sing, and keep your eyes on the road!

For those of you who have insanely busy schedules, it is very easy to put off practice until you have "enough time." We all know that enough time is, of course, never available, so it becomes a self-defeating issue. No time, no practice, no improvement, which creates feelings of frustration and failure. The whole process then becomes another stressor in an already stress-filled life. Don't do it to yourself! If you can't get the "optimum" practice time or place, use what you have available. *Take small bites!* Five minutes here, five minutes there *(even if it's in the car or shower)* adds up. It's important that you spend time everyday thinking about and experimenting with singing. Even if you just listen consciously you will begin to notice a change.

Everybody wishes they could magically improve their singing ability. We have a strong desire for instant gratification. But, singing is like any other skill; you have to work at it. If

The Zen of Singing ©

you don't do the work, you will not improve, so no excuses... just do it!

Basics

Start simply. Don't try to do that crazy difficult riff right out of the gate. Get the basic melody down first, and then add on. If you have trouble with a song, break the difficult phrases down and get clear on what is going on, but try to get in the habit of singing the songs all the way through. Don't constantly stop and start.

Think of sound as having shape, weight, and density. Become conscious of the shape and weight of every note. Is it a heavy, dense note or a light airy one? Is it round and rich or thin and wide? Experiment with the different sounds you can make. Get familiar with all of the possibilities of your sound palette; you never know what will come in handy and when.

Remember that good singing requires the coordination of support, vocal mechanism, and resonators.... PLUS the thoughtful engagement of your brain!

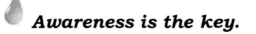 *Awareness is the key.*

Posture is a must for singing. If your body is collapsed in on itself you can't support the tone! Try these:

1. Imagine there is a hook attached to the crown of your head, and you are hanging from a string attached to the ceiling. *(Like a marionette.)*

2. Balance your head on your neck as if it were a pool ball on a cue stick

Tips

- Work through problem areas in your voice gently and consistently.

- Choose what to emphasize; don't fall into it by accident.

- When you open your mouth, KNOW what is going to come out.

- ALLOW yourself to sing...Don't force yourself.

Using Tape Recorders

We all flinch the first time we hear ourselves recorded and played back. No one ever sounds the way they expect to. It's normal to sound very different on tape than the way you hear yourself. You are used to hearing yourself from the perspective of inside your head, and it takes some getting used to. Sometimes the recorder itself distorts and otherwise affects the quality of our voice. Try not to be overly critical, stay objective, and listen for whatever technical aspect you are working on. With time and patience it will become more comfortable.

The Zen of Singing ©

Notes

_____

_____

_____

_____

_____

_____

_____

_____

_____

_____

_____

_____

The following page contains an exercise that I suggest you incorporate into your practice early on. Singing really requires coordinating a whole lot of things at one time: tone, breath, placement, melody, lyrics, dynamics, rhythm, phrasing, etc. Yikes!! Since we can't hold two new thoughts at one time, *(frankly, I have enough trouble with one new thing at a time...)* it becomes necessary for us to shift our attention back and forth between different aspects of singing.

I call this "The Scan."

Scan well...

Scan often...

The Zen of Singing ©

"The Scan"

There are so many things to think about when you are singing that this is a great little tool to help you check in with your body and make sure all is well. While you are singing, start at the top of your head and slowly move down your body. What's going on with the muscles in your face, jaw, neck, where are your shoulders, how about your tongue, how is your breathing and placement, and your pitch? As you discover problem spots, spend a moment with them and try to put things in order; then move on. It will be slow going at first, but the process gets faster and faster with time.

Work on your focus and awareness of details. Cover one thing at a time. Notice your relationship to it. For example: focus on volume. How does the tone you are singing fit into the picture? Are you singing loudly or softly? Change the volume and play with the dynamics. Do the same with pitch, tempo, and tone color.

Since you can't effectively hold 2 thoughts at a time, when you sing you should occasionally isolate each aspect of your delivery. For example, go through a song once to check the melody, again to check the breath, again to check the placement, another time for diction, and then dynamics. Then forget about everything but the feeling of the song. Clarify each aspect. Then try to integrate them as a whole.

Use

Your

Gifts...

The Zen of Singing ©

3. Range

One octave well sung trumps two poorly sung...

Range is the part of your voice in which you are most comfortable singing. It varies from person to person and is the result of your physical makeup. Some people who sing very low can also sing very high and visa versa, but they are the exceptions. Most people have a workable range of about two octaves. Remember, the operative word here is workable, the part of your voice that feels and sounds comfortable and natural, not the low notes you can scrape off the bottom or squeak out of the top end. You should work to expand your range, but approach it realistically. <u>The quality of the sound is much more important than how high or low it is.</u>

Allow your range to develop naturally, and don't try to push it beyond its comfort level right away. Some people get so hung up on wanting to sing high they forget the idea of quality. The goal is to have a consistent, supple, beautiful tone from one end of your range to the other. If you can sing a high C, great! But if it sounds strained and painful, what is the point? Being able to sing very high or low notes is only useful if they sound good. Work at building a strong, flexible range from the middle outward, and as you gain control and flexibility, you will find the extremes naturally follow suit.

Vocal coordination can be developed. Flexibility, volume, stamina, and texture choices can change, but your basic instrument is decided by your physiology. It will not change. "Expanding" your range is nothing more than learning to control and utilize what you already have. Save yourself, and everyone else, grief by accepting and developing your gifts. Don't waste your time being disappointed by what you don't have.

"The Break"
(Also called The Passagio or Passage)

You know that part of your voice that cracks and wobbles before it settles into that high fluty upper voice? That's the break. *(Good name, eh?)* Virtually everyone has a break. Some have learned to navigate it. Some just "flip" through it. Some find that they strain so hard they can't get through to the other side of it, and their voice stops at the break. Either way, it's the big boogie for singers and must be addressed. Here's the skinny.

Everyone has 3 parts to their range, low, medium, and high. Now, most people move back and forth with ease between the lower and middle register but find the transition between the middle register and the high register *(head voice in women, falsetto in men)* accompanied by sudden squeaks, cracking, and dynamic shifts or total cessation of sound.

The problem lies in learning to coordinate the action of the vocal cords through that transition. If you are pushing and straining until you can't squeak any higher and suddenly let go of the tension, you will flip into that head/falsetto sound. Not good! The goal is to smooth out the transition. Let it happen more gradually. If you learn to blend the tone and move into your head voice without that flip, you will get a richer sound during the process. Much easier said than done.

First, let go of the tension. Get the pressure off your vocal cords, so they can shift gracefully. Sing softly and keep the placement forward and high, out of your throat. At first your voice will probably sound weak and very disappointing, but give it time to adjust to the new usage, and you will

The Zen of Singing ©

surprise yourself. With time and work will come coordination, strength, and tone.

Work through your break high to low, back and forth, VERY gently, and only for short periods. This is a delicate part of your instrument, so don't ever push or strain when working through it. Humming gently from one end of your range to the other is also very useful.

Exercises for range include:

- Scales

- Octaves *(sliding)*

- Sighing and Intoning *(move from speech level sighing to singing.)*

In general, if you can't hum a tone or sing it softly, you shouldn't be trying to sing it full voice; however, sometimes it may seem easier to sing a high note loudly. This most likely means you are pushing to get to the note rather than using good technique. This may work for a while, but it is quite dangerous in the long run. A coordinated, supple instrument with good range combined with the dynamic possibilities of *support* will allow you to hit those high notes without abusing your vocal cords.

Connection

The connection between speaking and singing

We often speak at a pitch that is outside of our natural range. There can be many reasons for this, most of them unconscious. To sound powerful or sexy we may speak at a lower pitch. A higher pitch can communicate passivity or vulnerability. Perhaps we started emulating a hero when we were young and just kept the speech habit. Whatever the reason, if we speak outside of our natural tessitura *(range)* we are misusing our instrument, and it can cause us chronic problems with our voice. Hoarseness, sore throats, or vocal exhaustion may be the result. Singing is an extension of speech, so we are liable to manifest any bad speech habits we already have, plus add more in an attempt to compensate for the problems they cause.

Speaking and singing are different uses of the same instrument, so pay attention to how you use your voice. Get connected to what your voice FEELS like. Notice how it moves and changes depending upon your mood, energy level, and intention. Feel how excitement, tenderness, or anger changes the tone placement and the way you use your air.

To help you find your natural speaking range, try this:

- Laugh lightly and naturally. *(Ah Ha Ha ..not a belly laugh.)*
- Answer a question with, " hmmmm?" or "Uh- Huh"

You will probably notice that the pitch is higher than you expected and that you feel it in your face masque. That is the range you should be speaking in for optimum voice usage. It may sound or feel weird at first, but give it a try for a while, and you may be surprised at how much more comfortable speaking becomes. By adding breath control and placement to speech, you can project your voice with ease and clarity. This is a real boon for public speakers or those who speak a lot on their jobs, like teachers, lawyers, and actors. Once you get the hang of it, try the exercise on the following page.

The Zen of Singing ©

Speak a phrase or read something out loud:

1. Conversationally, as if you are sitting right next to someone

2. As if you are speaking to someone across the room

3. As if you are trying to be heard across the yard *(don't yell... focus and "project.")*

Always pay attention to how it feels. If it hurts or feels strained you are yelling or pushing. Rethink your approach and practice until it becomes easy and comfortable.

Tips

- **Your Key:** There is no such thing as a "one-size-fits-all" key. Different songs will lie in a different part of your optimal range *(tessitura)*. Judge your key for <u>each</u> song by comfort and sound, not math.

- Humming helps with high and low notes. If you can't hum a pitch or sing it quietly, don't try to sing it full voice by pushing it.

Range Chart

Range Finder

Chart **A** below shows the *approximate* ranges defined by the terms above them. Use chart **B** to graph your own range to get a sense of where you fit into the general standard of those terms. Also, make a note of where your break is. Remember, the charts are approximate. These are not ironclad rules, merely guidelines. Chart your progress as you continue to study and note your improvement. *(Just count real tones, not the squeaks or rumbles at the extremes.)*

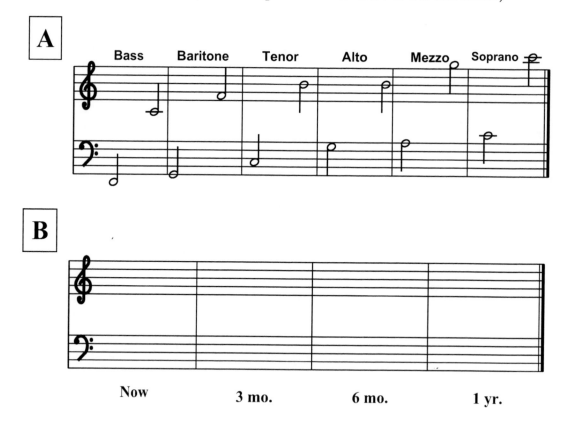

Now   3 mo.   6 mo.   1 yr.

The Zen of Singing ©

Notes

_____

_____

_____

_____

_____

_____

_____

_____

_____

_____

_____

_____

The Journey is one of

Self-Discovery,

The Reward is

Finding Your Voice...

4. Journaling

Discover and clarify through writing...

Start a Music/Singing Journal

Some people find keeping a journal easy, even natural. Others are resistant to it, but it's a useful learning tool, and I strongly suggest you incorporate it into your process. It's a revealing way to get in touch with your subconscious and perhaps deal with blocks associated with your singing or performance. It is also a good way to keep track of your progress, thoughts, questions, or any problems that may arise. If nothing else, it's a great place to set goals, list songs you would like to learn, do character studies, list music or CD's to check out, and comment about artists you like or dislike. It can be as simple as a few pages from a notebook or as elaborate as you care to make it. I suggest you choose one that draws you; makes you want to pick it up and write. If it bores or intimidates you, you will avoid it. However, don't let the lack of the perfect journal become an excuse to keep you from beginning.

The first time you sit down and try it you may feel silly or think you don't have anything to say. That's O.K. Write down whatever comes into your mind. If that is, "I feel silly" or, "I just have nothing to say", write it down. Then write the question "Why do I feel silly?" Sit quietly and think about the question for a moment, and then write down the next thing that pops into your mind, no matter what it is. Keep at this for a while. You may end up with a page of absolute gibberish, but you will be starting the dialogue, which is, in fact, all journaling is, having a dialogue with yourself. Eventually, after you wade through all the "this is stupid" or, "I can't think of anything to say" stuff, you are liable to get to something interesting, especially if you respond to the statements with a question and then try to answer that question honestly.

It is very important that you feel safe to express yourself in the journal. It is private, and you don't need to share it with anyone unless you want to. Don't worry about spelling or grammar. Don't worry about form or penmanship. Just write whatever comes to mind, silly, brilliant, or merely mundane... a few cryptic words or pages and pages of longhand. It's all useful one way or another as a means of self-discovery. That brings us back to the central idea of a journey to consciousness.

Exercises

1. Make a list of songs you would like to learn. What do you like about them?

2. List songs or singers you like. Why do you like them?

3. List songs or singers you don't like. Why don't you like them?

4. Make notes about things you have either trouble or success with during your practice or performance. For example, difficult notes or phrases or trouble with lyrics or delivery. Notice any patterns?

5. Do you notice that some days singing is easier than others? If so, make notes about what is going on, tension, rest, diet, allergies, etc. How do these things affect you? Again, notice any patterns.

The Zen of Singing ©

Further work

Journaling is a great tool for self-discovery. Use it to explore your feelings about singing, music, performance, and practice. Do you tend to accept and deal with challenges, or is your first response to something new or difficult, "I can't do this!"? If so, why do you think that is? Do you remember any occasions when you were made to feel bad about your voice or, wanting to sing or perform, perhaps a thoughtless word from a family member, friend, or teacher, which you found particularly painful? Are there any occasions when you recall truly enjoying singing or performing? Sit down and allow the memories to come. Then go back and read what you have written. See if anything emerges as a turning point or a pattern. If so, explore it.

One more thing, go back and read your journal occasionally, from the beginning. It will give you a sense of the progress you have made, which you may otherwise not even notice. I'll bet you will be surprised by the problems you solve, the questions you've answered, and the things you've learned about yourself!

<u>Replace the Inner Critic</u>

<u>with</u>

<u>the Observer</u>

You know that little voice that is always yammering at you about how "You can't", "If you were any good you would already know this or could already do this", or "What if I blow it?" etc. Well, meet your Inner Critic. Sometimes it merely keeps us on track, but often it just gets in our way and overwhelms us with doubt. Creating situations we cannot solve because we are too busy focusing on the darned voice!

For our journey, we need to replace that little voice with a new one. The Observer. The Observer is curious and objectively gathers information about what is going on. He/she does NOT judge, merely notices and makes note of.

The Inner Critic is a block… The Observer is a bridge.

The Zen of Singing ©

Notes

_____

_____

_____

_____

_____

_____

_____

_____

_____

_____

_____

_____

Your Breath

Is Your Life...

The Zen of Singing ©

5. Breathing

Control, not quantity...

Breathing is the centerpiece of your support. The ability to control and direct your breath is as important as your ability to breathe deeply. You need to incorporate a natural breathing technique with a certain amount of conscious manipulation in order to get the best results. Good technique requires the coordination of breath and sound, not just the ability to inhale and expel large amounts of air.

Consider how easily your unconscious controls the airflow needed for conversation. There is rarely intervention on your part. You have some idea of what is necessary, and your body automatically adjusts to the requirements. It's much like walking. You need to know in what direction you are moving and how quickly or slowly you need to get there, but you are normally not concerned with exactly which muscles are involved in the process. That will happen when you sing as well, as long as you have a clear idea of what you need and how to get it. Once you have a firm grasp of how to use your diaphragm correctly, just relax and let your body do what it knows to do.

Contrary to the belief of many beginning singers, it doesn't require large quantities of air moving in and out of your mouth to make sound. What is does require is control of air pressure. Imagine a balloon. If you blow the balloon up air pressure builds up inside of it. By using your fingers and thumbs as a valve, you can cause the escaping air to sound a pitch. As the air escapes the pressure drops, so to maintain consistent air pressure you would have to squeeze *(or support)* the balloon.

That is basically what happens when you sing. The air pressure builds up behind your vocal cords and disperses after it gets past them. If you are still blowing air after that happens or if you are blowing too much air, you get a breathy, unclear sound. A breathy quality to singing is much like whispering is to speaking. It may occasionally be an interesting effect, but you certainly don't want to be stuck with that sound.

Since breathing is usually an unconscious act, you have probably not thought much about it, except for those times when illness, exhaustion, or external sources such as smog or changes in air pressure make it difficult. Although it is normally controlled unconsciously, it is fairly easy to gain conscious control of it. Besides providing your lungs with life sustaining air, breathing also serves as a barometer for what is going on in your body. If you are stressed, the center of your breath is high. As you go about your normal daily tasks your breathing tends to be centered in your chest, which keeps you alert, yet not stressed. As you relax, the centers of your breathing drops lower and lower until you are in a fully relaxed state, and your breathing is then controlled by your diaphragm. *(Watch a sleeping baby's tummy as they breathe...)*

The diaphragm is a dome shaped muscle that bisects your body, separating your heart and lungs from the rest of your organs. As you inhale deeply it drops down and out, moving your organs out of the way and allowing the air to get to the lower part of your lungs. As you exhale, it contracts back into its original position. Pretend you have a balloon in your stomach. When you inhale you fill the balloon with air, and your stomach expands. When you exhale you empty the balloon of air, and your stomach contracts.

The Zen of Singing ©

Observe ~ Understand ~ Manipulate

Learning anything occurs in stages. First you must _Observe_, " What is" to become conscious of or discover something. Then you must assess it so that you can _Understand_ or make sense of it. Only then can you _Manipulate_ or change it effectively. Since breathing is a natural function, it is important that you observe it in its natural state and not merely try to imagine what you _think_ correct breathing is. To that end, the first thing you have to do is objectively observe yourself breathing in many different circumstances.

Start by observing your breathing at different times throughout the day, when at rest, working, stressed, etc. What does it feel like? Where is it centered? What muscles are moving and in which direction? Really work to get a sense of what it FEELS like as a whole body experience. For example, when you breathe deeply you will obviously feel it in your upper abdomen and chest, but what about your back? What about your lower abdomen? When you take a really deep, relaxed breath can you feel it down in your legs? _(Obviously you are not feeling air in your legs. What you are feeling is a relaxing of those muscles in response to the breath.)_ Get to know what is going on in your body when you breathe. Only when your conscious mind has a clear understanding of what it wants will the unconscious mind allow it to take over this job effectively. Otherwise, you have both sides at odds, and major confusion is the result. Your body WANTS to give you what you ask of it. That's its job, but if you don't ask clearly and in a way that it understands, it will automatically default to your subconscious and ignore you, much like a computer.

Hold your hand up, flat, palm in, about 3 inches from your mouth and see how much air you feel moving while singing scales on "ah". You should feel little, if any. You can also try using a candle held about 6 inches from your mouth. When you sing the flame should not jump around. Once you are clear about the amount of air really necessary to get

the job done we can move on to controlling that air. Once
again...

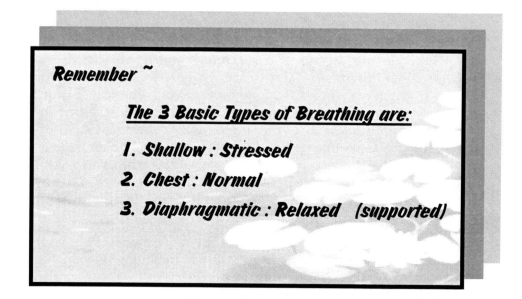 **Awareness is the key.**

Relaxation and visualization are great tools. Also investi-
gate Yoga and meditation breathing. These forms of breathing contain many of the skills we use and will help you become conscious of the process. The more control you have
over your breath, the better off you will be.

Remember ~

The 3 Basic Types of Breathing are:

1. Shallow : Stressed

2. Chest : Normal

3. Diaphragmatic : Relaxed (supported)

Experience Your Breath

Visualization 1
(Exercise on CD)

Lie flat, arms relaxed beside you, palms up. Close your eyes and focus on your breathing. Don't try to control it; just notice it objectively. Now, tighten your entire body up and tense your muscles as much as possible. Hold it for the count of 3; then suddenly let ALL of the tension go. Rest for a moment and do it again once or twice.

Now rest a few moments and again notice your breathing...

When you feel ready, imagine that it is a sunny, warm, beautiful day, and you are either lying at the beach, or some favorite spot. Really try to see, hear, and feel the place. What does the sun feel like? What sounds accompany this special place?

Allow the sun to warm you gently, and imagine that all of your stress and tension are melting like warm butter into the ground, your body feeling light and weightless. Stay in this relaxed state and observe your breathing. Put your right hand on your stomach at about the navel. If you are fully relaxed, this is the area that will feel like the center of your breathing. *(Instead of high in your chest.)* Relax and experience your breathing for a while.

Now put your left hand on your stomach below your other hand, just between the pelvic bones, and take a deeper breath. Can you feel both hands moving? This is what diaphragmatic breathing feels like. Your whole torso is involved. Relax and experience it as fully as possible. Notice what muscles are moving and in which direction. What do you feel in your side? Notice what is going on in your lower back.

Your shoulders should not be moving towards your ears. When you inhale your tummy should move towards the ceiling. When you exhale it should move back down towards the floor. If this is not the case, you are not relaxed enough. Don't worry; you will get it with practice.

As you begin to feel confident that you fully understand what is moving, and how, slowly sit up, keeping you breath centered as low as you can. It will want to creep back up as gravity and awareness shifts, but try to override that instinct. Lean over and put your elbows near your knees and continue to breathe. This will help you feel it in your lower back.

When you feel ready, slowly stand up, continuing to monitor your breath and trying to keep it centered low in your belly. It will probably have sneaked right back up into your chest, but with practice you will be able to move it at will. After all, breathing is pretty darned important, you wouldn't want your unconscious mind to give your conscious mind control until it was pretty sure you wouldn't make a muck of it, would you?

Support

Remember that support is the use and control of air pressure, NOT merely sucking and blowing lots of air. Clean sound requires the control and coordination of your breath with the finite motor muscles of your vocal mechanism. It's much like using a clutch. There is an almost inexplicable connection and coordination that takes place between your gas pedal foot and your clutch foot that only comes with practice and work. Like a clutch, your action must be smooth and connected.

Try to imagine a column of water shooting straight up from a fountain, like a geyser. Now imagine a ping pong ball balanced on top of it. If the water pressure drops, so does the ball. If there is too much pressure the ball flies away, out of control. If the column diffuses and is no longer focused, it can't hold the ball up at all. If the support is not steady and focused, the tone is unstable.

Belly Breathing *(Your Powerhouse)*

We are usually encouraged to "tuck that gut in" or "tighten those abs!" so it's no wonder we are so resistant to letting our belly relax or release. Well, to really support our singing we need to adopt what I call "Goddess" or " Buddha Belly" Instead of holding those muscles tight, we need to let them go to breathe deeply. If you release those muscles it moves your guts out of the way so that the lower part of your lungs can fill. Since nature abhors a vacuum, the air will naturally move into your lungs to equalize the air pressure. Voila'... more air, less strain.

Once you drop your belly to get the air in, then you put it back in place as you exhale. So instead of collapsing your chest to squeeze air out from the top down, which cuts off all access to your support, you use your diaphragm to control the air and support the tone. This is your "Power-house" of support. Support will make the difference between a big, relaxed, lifted sound, and a tight, pinched, yelling sound. Collapsing your chest is like squeezing toothpaste from the top of the tube.

Imagine a nice fat water balloon. When you fill it from the tap it fills from the bottom and expands. Right? Imagine that your belly is that balloon, and as you inhale it is filling from the bottom up. Now imagine you set the balloon flat in the palm of your hand and give it a quick, but gentle squeeze. The water would squirt out of the top, wouldn't it? That's the kind of thing you are doing with your breath.

The Zen of Singing ©

Tips

1. "Allow" yourself to breathe. Don't try to force it or "suck" air. Breathe in response to relaxing.

2. The lower your breathing is centered, the more relaxed you are. Conversely, the higher the center, the more stressed.

3. Be sure the muscle motion is "connected " to the breath. Don't just shove your muscles in and out.

4. When singing you will usually breathe through your mouth. *(Quietly!)*

5. Match your breath intake to the phrases. *(i.e.: short phrase = shorter breath, long phrase = deeper breath.)* You do this naturally when you speak, so let it become natural when you sing.

6. DON'T LET YOUR CHEST COLLAPSE!!! When your lungs get to be about 1/2 empty your chest will naturally start to collapse... Don't let it. Hold it open.

Finding Your Diaphragm

Uh oh... THE DIAPHRAGM. *(Scary music, please...)* That ever mysterious and always slightly intimidating "THING", as in, "No, no you must sing from your diaphragm! " *(Huh??)* Quite simply, it's a sheet muscle that separates your lower chest cavity from your upper chest cavity. It's shaped like a dome, or a mushroom, and it moves up and down as well as in and out.

To find that little puppy, pretend you are blowing out a candle with a short, quick breath. Feel that little contraction? Well, there you have it. Meet your diaphragm and make friends with it. Get to be good intimate friends, because you will need to learn to work together from now on. Another way to find your diaphragm is to "HSSSSS" like a snake. Yep, there it is again. Kind of a cute litter bugger, eh?

That little contraction you feel is called an "attack". Keep that in mind, as you will be hearing that word a lot. The attack is merely the way you start the sound. The source of the attack has MUCH to do with the resulting sound and your control of it.

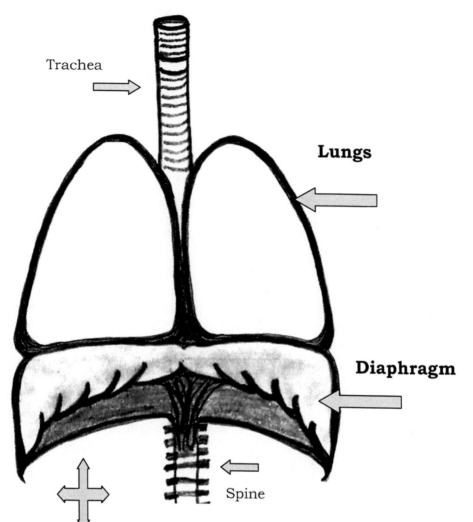

Trachea

Lungs

Diaphragm

Spine

Other Stuff:
Intestines, Stomach, Liver, etc...

When you inhale the diaphragm expands down and out, *moving your intestines out of the way and making room for the lower lobes of your lungs to fill.*

Figure 1 Diaphragm

Exercises

(In no particular order. Find some that work for you.)

1. Count 1-10 slowly in a monotone. Then forcefully blow whatever air you have left out on " SSSSS". *(Like a snake)*

2. Inhale 3 counts - Hold 3 counts - exhale 6 counts. *(Slowly)*

3. Pant like a dog. If you have trouble, start slowly and pretend that you are blowing out a candle. Inhale expanding your lower belly. Then blow hard and exhale quickly. Speed up until it becomes panting. *Tip:* Give your tummy a little squeeze when you exhale and release it when you inhale.

4. Sing "HA" staccato on the scale degrees 1-3-5-8-5-3-1. Feel that squeeze? Be sure to release your diaphragm between each note.

5. Lie down and put a book *(not too heavy)* on your belly. Relax and breath so that you make it rise toward the ceiling as you inhale, and fall towards the floor as you exhale.

6. Count to 50 softly on a note. *(Singing softly forces you to control the breath.)*

7. Take a breath and expand your ribs. Wide like a barrel, not raising your shoulders. Tie a rope around your ribcage in this expanded state and then breathe, trying to keep the rope tight around your ribs. Keep your ribs open and use your tummy to do the work.

The Zen of Singing ©

8. Say the alphabet as many times as possible on a single breath.

9. Hold something heavy over your head and inhale.

10. Sing a note on "VVV". *(Also good for Placement)*

11. Place your hands on your ribs. Expand your ribs, pushing them against your hands when you inhale.

Experiment a lot! The more you observe and become aware of your breath, the more easily you will find it to control consciously. Use breathing to calm down, by slowing it and dropping the center into your belly. Use it to wake up by taking short, shallow breaths. Generally speaking, we could all use more oxygen... so breathe, folks, breathe!

Using a mirror to monitor yourself

Often bad habits become such a part of our sense of normal that we no longer feel them. Practice using a mirror, and you will see many things you may not feel. We are very adaptable creatures. For example, let's say you carry a lot of tension in your shoulders, so much and so often that the feeling of tension becomes normal, and you are not aware that you shoulders are pulled up, but if you look in a mirror you can see that they are up around your ears!

The mirror can be a great ally. One word of advice though, if you have a tendency to giggle or feel silly when you look at yourself in a mirror, avoid looking into your own eyes. Focus on the part of your face or body you are working on.

The mirror is great tools...use it!

The Zen of Singing ©

Notes

_____

_____

_____

_____

_____

_____

_____

_____

_____

_____

_____

_____

_____

You are the Resonator,

Create the Shape

Of the Sound...

6. Placement, Control, and Attack

Resonance changes everything...

Placement

Placement is a very abstract concept; since it involves the way you experience your own body. It is the spot where you feel the center of the sound, not all the attendant vibrations and overtones. It can border on crazy making to try and explain, so let's try a few exercises and see if you can feel it.

Start with speaking. Go back and read the previous paragraph out loud. Where do you feel the sound? In your throat? Front or back? In your head? *(Hint: It moves around naturally, so you will probably feel it in a lot of places.)*

Do not think of placement as being something you force or push. For our purposes we will call it the effective use of our resonators. In the natural course of using your voice you will notice that it moves all over the place depending on the vowel or consonant sounds, inflection, and where it is " pitched". *(Meaning how high or low the sound is.)* For example, say the vowel "AH" several times. Try to get clear about where you feel it focused. Now say "EE". Feel the difference? Put them together and say "AH –EE". Now do you feel it? Try it pitched higher, then pitch it lower. I call this finding where the sound "lives", the place it naturally or habitually goes. Play with all the vowel sounds and find their natural homes. Add some consonants. Try: " Ta, La, Na, Fa, Da, Ga". Feel the differences? Now try "Ta-Ti", "La-

Li", "Ga-Gi". Feel it? Get familiar with these habitual spots. Getting connected to the sense of where your voice is and why it is there will help you choose where you want to focus the sound. *(If you have trouble try working with your eyes closed.)*

Notice how far down your throat "AH" is and how much more forward "EE" is? Really feel the difference. Now, put a cork between your teeth, *(or two fingers)* and say it again. Do you feel all the different possibilities? What we want to do as singers is to make choices about where things should " live", rather than just rely on chance.

To get an idea of where a "forward" sound is exhale through your nose, then sniff in, and then hum. (Hum on M, N, or NG.)

Figure 2 Face Masque Placement

Try This:

Make a "V" with your index and middle finger. Place one finger on each side of your face. *(Right next to, and just below your nostrils)* Now gently lift and separate. Say "AH" and "EE" again.

Feel the difference?

By moving the *"center"* *(or "focus")* of the sound out of the back of your throat and into your face masque, you are using your natural resonators to develop the sound. You are not forcing or straining from your throat. The sound is much easier to produce and easier to control.

If you have trouble getting the tone forward, close your eyes and touch the spot between your eyebrows. *(This brings your attention to that area)* When you sing "Intend" the tone into that spot, high and forward in your face masque.

Open Throat

You may have heard this term before. Teachers will often say, " open the throat!" but what the heck does it mean? Well, for pop singing it does *not* mean expanding your throat like a bullfrog! *(For classical singing, well, that is an argument for another day.)* A <u>pushed</u> open throat gives you the Pee Wee Herman sound. Not to mention, it puts major strain on your instrument!

To find an open throat, relax and try to smell the skin on your arm. No harsh sniffing; actually try to catch your scent. To do this everything has to relax and open. The soft palette lifts and the tongue and larynx drop a bit. Now THAT is an open throat!

Resonators

Resonation is the way in which a tone is amplified acoustically. Our body is our resonator. Certain parts of our bodies do the job more effectively than others. Like a piano, it requires hard surfaces and empty space so the vibrations created by the tone can have room to develop and conduct the sound. Soft tissue is not a good resonator. Our primary resonators are the mouth cavity and sinus areas. Our chest can resonate sympathetically, especially on low notes, but the throat is not a very effective resonator. *(Even if you do the Bullfrog thing!)*

Imagine an acoustic guitar...

The Zen of Singing ©

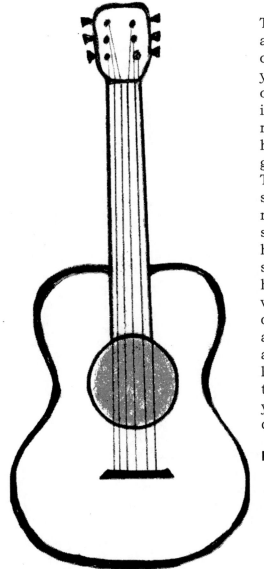

The strings create the pitch and the body of the guitar creates the resonation. If you cover the hole in the face of the guitar you eliminate it's primary source of resonation, and you have to hit the strings VERY hard to get any volume out of them. Too much of that and the strings will break, not to mention the lack of tone subtleties. With the sound hole open, the strings can be strummed gently and still have a great amount of volume. That is MUCH easier on the strings. The strings are like your vocal cords, and the body of the guitar is like your resonators. Learn to use them effectively, and you will be less likely to damage them.

Figure 3 Guitar

The shape of the resonator determines the shape of the sound.

Learn to visualize the sound. Think of it as having shape, weight, and density. Design the sound you want and aim it.

An oval sound is round and rich:

A Horizontal sound is broad and narrow:

Most people envision singing as something that starts in your throat and comes out of your mouth. That is a very limiting idea and forces your throat to work MUCH too hard. From now on think of singing as a "whole body" event and work to keep the tone out of your throat. I find it helpful to imagine that the sound is coming up the back of my spine and neck, and then moving out through my face masque. *(The area above the roof of your mouth)* Learn to place the tone high and forward in your face masque. Don't sing **from** the throat; sing **thru** it.

There is a bridge between speaking and singing. Good singing should be as natural as speaking. In speech we aim at the consonants. In singing we aim at the vowels. You can learn to see the connection between the two by intoning. Say "MAW" in a natural voice, about the middle of your range. Say it a few times and get a feel for it. Now stretch the "AW" out a little bit. " MAAAW" Do it a few more times until you are stretching the vowel and it begins to sound like a tone. " MAAAAAAAAAAAAW" Do this gently, and don't push, force, or growl.

Relax... experiment... observe.

The Zen of Singing ©

Exercises – Placement

1. Hum... feel the vibration high in your face masque.

2. Hum to place the sound forward. Then, holding the sound forward, and lingering on the MMM sound, sing: "**M**AW **M**AY **M**EE **M**OW **M**OO".

3. Lean forward, head dropped towards your knees, while singing "**N**I **N**I **N**I". *(Overemphasize the "N")*

4. Talk like The Coneheads from Saturday Night Live.

5. "Beep Beep" like the Roadrunner *(cartoon character)*.

Don't let your throat get tight. A nice relaxed sigh on "AAAAHHH" will help open the back of your throat.

Control

Control is not as in tight, or tense, or control-freak! We are talking about a relaxed awareness of what you are doing and an ability to make good technique choices. Consistency is really important here. If your tone is iffy or bouncing all over the map, you will loose the clarity and flow of the music.

Air pressure and placement must remain consistent. Remember, you should choose your sound, don't just open your mouth and hope something good comes out. Know what will come out!

Exercises- Control

1. Choose one note and sing a vowel "Messa di Voce". *(This is Crescendo - Decrescendo on long tones. No vibrato until the end please.)*

2. Legato Intervals: Deliberate Gilssando *(Slide)* up and down 3rds, 5ths & Octaves. Start slow then speed up.

3. Experiment with the way you use vibrato. Practice singing with no vibrato. Add it by choice. Try not to fall into the overuse of it.

Attack

This is simply how you start the tone. Even though we use the word " Attack", it should be done gently. Try not to slam your poor vocal cords around. Get conscious of your initial attack: Where is it coming from? Your throat? Your diaphragm? Also, pay attention to how precise it is. Don't slide up or down to pitches or from the consonants to the vowels. Your tongue should be relaxed, fairly flat, and out of the way, no tension, pulling, scooping in the middle, or sticking out of your mouth.

Keep the pressure <u>off</u> your vocal cords.

Tips

1.   <u>Avoid</u>: ***Explosive*** attacks: A sudden burst of air forcing the cords to open suddenly and slam back together.

2.   <u>Avoid</u>: ***Breathy*** attacks: Too much air. Avoid starting words with an extra "H" sound at the beginning, or adding one in the middle of a word.

Understand

Your

Instrument...

The Zen of Singing ©

7. Vocal Cords

Allow them do their job without interference...

Your vocal cords are muscles that stretch from the front to the back of the throat. They are located behind your "Adams Apple", *(which is really your Thyroid Cartilage)* in your voice box *(the Larynx)*. Singing requires using airflow to co-ordinate the vocal cords with all the other muscles in the larynx. Then you have to coordinate the voice box with your support and placement.

To sing effectively you need to learn to RELAX your throat/neck. Tension adversely affects the vocal cords ability to do their job. Tight throat muscles push and pull your larynx and cause strain. Learn to feel tension and let go of it. Replace the habit of tension with the habit of relaxation. Learn "Non - Effort"

Your throat should not be closed and tight nor pushed open like a bullfrog's. Both create strain. Use the "Smelling your skin" exercise to open your throat. You should feel your tongue relax and your soft palate lift. Your chewing muscles, jaw, and larynx also relax. Singing from this position should feel very comfortable. If your soft palate is lowered or tensed it will cause a nasal sound. A tight tongue or jaw will change vowel sounds *("ah" becomes more like "uh")*. Both cause strain.

Your tongue should be relaxed and down. Touch your Adams apple and start shoving your tongue around, and you will see how what you do with your tongue affects your voice box. They are attached! Your tongue is an important player. Pay attention to how you use it and what it is doing. Notice how it moves and any tension you feel. Is it arching or scooping in the middle? Is it pulled up at the back?

Relax your tongue, don't let it pull up in back, stick out the front of your mouth, or scoop in the middle. Also, don't hold it down or try to force it into place. Let it relax into place. Try saying "Koo Koo Koo" and notice how your tongue feels when it lowers in back.

Run your tongue back from the Hard Palate behind your front teeth until you feel it get soft and smooth. That's your Soft Palate; it ends with that dangly thing, which is your Uvula.

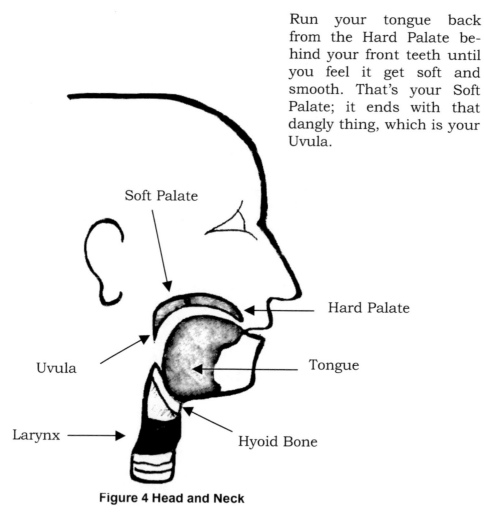

Figure 4 Head and Neck

The Zen of Singing ©

Connections

Your tongue is a <u>big</u> player. Notice how it is connected to your Hyoid Bone, which is connected to your Voice Box. So, if your tongue is tense or pulling, it's pulling your poor voice box all over the place!

(Hmmm. "Your arm bone's connected to your shoulder bone...")

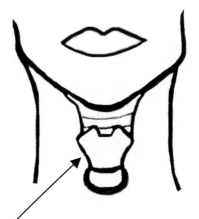

Thyroid Cartilage
(Also known as your *Adam's Apple*. The Larynx is behind it)

Figure 5 Thyroid Cartilage

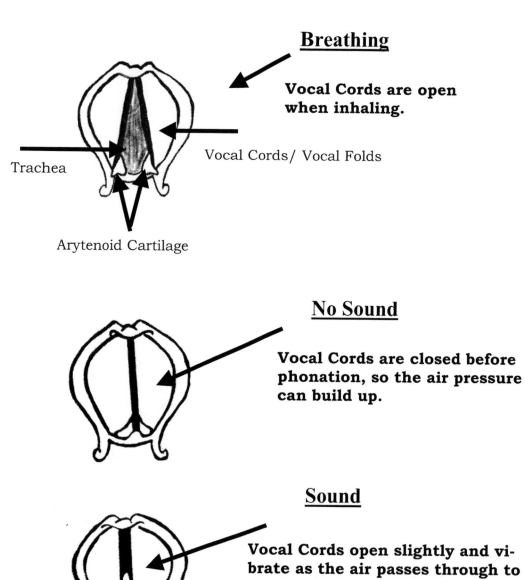

Breathing

Vocal Cords are open when inhaling.

Vocal Cords/ Vocal Folds

Trachea

Arytenoid Cartilage

No Sound

Vocal Cords are closed before phonation, so the air pressure can build up.

Sound

Vocal Cords open slightly and vibrate as the air passes through to create pitch. This happens many times per second, depending upon the note.

Figure 6 Vocal Cords

The Zen of Singing ©

Tongue Tension

To check the level of tension in your tongue, lay your index finger across your chin and push your thumb firmly up under your chin. Now sing a note. The degree to which your tongue pushes against your thumb will tell you how much tension you carry there.

A light pulse is normal, but if it tightens up or pushes hard, break the tension by pushing back hard with your thumb.

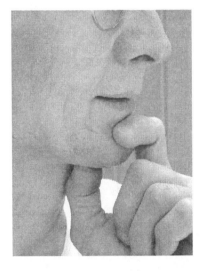

Figure 7 Tongue Tension Profile

Try This!

Using your thumb to monitor the action, hold your chin with your index finger, and put your thumb under your chin.

Push it up there and see how hard your tongue pulses against it when you sing your exercises.

If it pushes hard, that is a clue that your tongue is too tense!

Tips

- Your vocal cords need to stay hydrated. Like your eyes, if they dry out they get irritated and inflamed. Steam is great!

- Mucus protects your cords when they dry out or swell up, so if you have a lot of phlegm try to find out what's going on.

- DRINK LOTS OF WATER! It thins out mucus, and a well hydrated body works better overall.

- Try pretending you've just gotten a shot of Novocain and your tongue and jaw are slack *(play at talking & singing like this, don't worry about pronunciation)*

The Zen of Singing ©

Singing Sick

Oh... the thought can be terrifying! You have a gig tomorrow and you have no voice today. What to do? The first line of defense is, of course, to be good to your voice so that you don't loose it in the first place. Plenty of rest, fluids, no yelling or over-singing, no hard partying, etc...That said, we all get sick now and then, and for some reason the bugs just LOVE to plant themselves in a singers upper respiratory system!

Good technique can help you sing over a cold, unless it's in your lungs or causes serious laryngitis. Coughing aggravates the inflamed vocal chords, so the first thing is to get that cough stopped! Talk to your Doctor or Pharmacist about the appropriate cough meds. Do be careful taking ANY kind of cold or flu meds as the decongestants will dry you out. Great for the cold, lousy for singing...

There are many over-the-counter remedies available for throat problems, from herbal teas and lozenges to gargles, drops and atomizers. Check your health food stores and experiment to find what works best for you. Pay attention to any environmental or food issues that may be triggering vocal trouble. Pizza or ice cream before a gig is probably not the best choice. Smog, smoke, Santa Ana winds or chemicals at work may also be the source of vocal problems.

Your body needs to stay hydrated to work well, including vocally, so drink LOTS of water! *(It also helps thin out the mucus that can get stuck in your throat because of allergies or illness.)* Steam is a singer's friend. A nice long shower, or a few minutes with a personal vaporizer can really help if the vocal issues are related to dryness. Also, sleeping with a humidifier or vaporizer, especially during windy or cold conditions, can be a great help.

If you get a cold or flu do the usual, rest, fluids, stay warm, and... Shut up! Vocal Rest is the best favor you can do yourself. This means no singing or talking, especially whispering! Before you go to the gig, do an extra long warm up, VERY gently. Once you get to the gig make sure you have adequate monitors. Avoid cold drinks and anything that will dry you out, stick with soothing warm drinks and lozenges. Do not oversing... it will tear your voice up and it will take days to recover. The odds are that no one will even know you aren't in top shape if you don't tell them. Trust me, even if you do squeak or rasp a bit, it's not career ending.

If your voice is in *really* bad shape your Doctor may consider giving you steroids, but that's a pretty bad merry-go-round to hop on. If it's not a HUGE, life changing gig, send in a sub or cancel the date. Your long-term vocal health is much more important.

The Zen of Singing ©

Tips

- Vocal Rest is a singer's best friend.

- Notice how what you eat affects your voice *(dairy, for example)* and avoid things that cause problems at least 48 hours before a performance.

- Breathing steam is a singer's 2nd best friend

- Zinc lozenges are helpful for sore throats

- If you dry out when you sing, from nerves or food, there are a number of throat sprays on the market that can help. *(Never take the kind that numbs your throat.)*

- Cough drops and various throat-coating teas are also great.

- *Cyclone Cider* drops really help clear my throat, but watch out, they have a kick! *(Available at some health food stores)*

- Sleeping with a vaporizer or humidifier can be helpful if dry weather affects you.

You Must Be Heard

And

Understood...

The Zen of Singing ©

8. Articulation

Clarity and consonants ...

An important, yet often overlooked aspect of singing is articulation. *(The clarity with which we pronounce words.)* Obviously we want the sound we make to be beautiful and strong, but a song also has a lyrical content that adds greatly to the overall experience. Making beautiful sounds that no one can understand can seriously lessen the impact of the performance.

We have discussed the idea that different vowels and consonants naturally live in different places. Pay attention to them. Don't say "uh" when you should be saying "*ah*". Remember that words are not just a bunch of vowels strung together, so for goodness sake use the consonants! Sing on the vowel sound and articulate the consonants quickly and cleanly. While certain styles may call for variations, do it by choice, not by inattention. Communication is the thing, so be as clear as possible.

Flexibility and a light touch are the keys to good articulation. You may have to over emphasize certain consonant sounds slightly, which will probably feel strange at first, but it will make the words easier to understand in the context of a phrase. Be careful not to overdo it. That will make the phrases sound choppy or awkward. Use a tape recorder when you practice so that you can make sure that you are making the sound that you think you are making.

Practice over articulating, and then relax. <u>Work your tongue and lips, not your jaw.</u>

- Diphthongs: *(compound vowels)* Hold the first vowel sound. For example "Night" should be "NAAAH -ET" not "NAH-EEEET".

- Avoid adding an extra vowel sound to words: Down should not be Down-uh. Mine, not Mine-uh etc.

- Consonants should be clear and crisp. Get off of them quickly, and be sure they are pitched correctly.

Exercises

Your jaw should be relaxed. Don't let your tongue pull up in back, down in the middle, or stick out of your mouth. Use a tape recorder to check your progress.

1. Hold your tongue and read out loud. Enunciate clearly.

2. Roll the "R" as in Spanish. It requires a little flipping motion of the tongue right behind the front teeth. It sounds like a cat purring.

3. Work the tongue. Try words like: Melody, Hello, Yellow, Leather, Unique, New York. Over enunciate.

The Zen of Singing ©

Notes

Less Effort,

More Freedom...

The Zen of Singing ©

9. Relaxation

If there's tension in your mind or body, it is also in your voice...

The idea of relaxation during singing may seem impossible. What could be more stressful than standing up in front of a group of people and performing? Nonetheless, relaxation is a MUST if you intend to allow your voice to reach its potential. Stress, whether mental or physical, is an obstacle to using your instrument effectively and needs to be addressed.

Physical Stress

It should be obvious to you that physical stress creates problems with your ability to function. Just take a look at your breathing when you are upset, or the tightness you carry in your muscles. Tension in your body interferes with almost everything, including singing and performance.

Try to become aware of the ways your body carries stress. Do you tighten or clench your jaw? How about your tongue? Do your shoulders tighten and rise up around your ears? Do you feel sick to your stomach or have trouble breathing deeply? Sometimes we get so used to these feelings we adjust to them and compensate in other ways, completely unaware of the problem. Unfortunately, the ways in which we learn to compensate often create more problems!

It is important to pay close attention to your body and become aware of how stress affects you. Learn to relax completely and use that as a baseline from which to judge what's going on.

There are many techniques to help you, including:

- Meditation
- Visualization
- Stretching
- Bio-feedback
- Yoga
- Massage
- Prayer

Find something that works for you, and make it part of your routine. Your instrument will thank you!

Mental stress

Mental stress is much more insidious. While it usually manifests itself physically, the real damage is emotional. You know, those voices in our heads that say, " you can't do this", "you're no good", "you'll never get thru this", and on and on. *(Chapter 11, Performance Anxiety)* Some of these voices have roots in our childhood. Some may be born of more recent experiences. All of them get in the way of our ability to function.

First, you must become aware of them on a conscious level. Don't just let that stuff float around and ignore it. When you notice that negative self talk, stop it! Literally, just say, " stop!" every time you hear it. Eventually we want to replace those old nasty worn out tapes with some new, positive information, but if that's too much of a stretch for the moment, just say, "stop!" Discover and address how the negative talk manifests in your body, and do some work on your head so that you can take back control. Your harshest critic is usually you, so lighten up and give yourself a break!

Useful tools along the way can be:

- Journaling
- Self-help books
- Counseling
- Talking to friends
- Mentors
- Teachers

Remember, since your body is your instrument, learning to sing is truly a journey of self-discovery! Try journaling about any emotional issues that may be interfering with your ability to "be in" or relate to, your body. Pay attention to the way your emotions manifest physically. Whatever is going on in your head is going on in your body.

Become aware of this part of the equation. As you learn to relax your singing will improve, and you will probably see benefits in other parts of your life. Do the work. You'll be glad you did!

Exercises

These are some simple physical ways to relax and deal with stress.

- Physical warm up: Light stretches & bending. Neck circles & stretching your neck gently side to side

- Sighing gently on "*ah*" releases the jaw and throat muscles.

- Yawning

- Say *"Bumblebee"* as if you've had your mouth shot full of Novocain. Let your mouth go slack.

- Bubble your lips and make a sound like a motorboat.

- Relax and allow your larynx to lower. Don't push it. Just allow it to feel heavy and let go.

- Sit or lie comfortably, close your eyes, allow the center of your breathing to drop, and count your breaths

- Explore visualization as a relaxation tool.

The Zen of Singing ©

Notes

_____

_____

_____

_____

_____

_____

_____

_____

_____

_____

_____

_____

Let the Music

Teach You...

The Zen of Singing ©

10. The "Art" and "Craft" of Singing

A vocalist must be flexible, aware, focused, fearless, and in love with the process, both in performance and in life.

Basics

There are basically two ways to approach singing as performance, internally or externally. Much like acting, you can either "block" it out *(plan the movement, expression, and dynamics ahead of time)*, or you can "get into character" and trust that where it leads you is the right place. There are often situations when you will need to use both techniques. As a performer you will need to be comfortable with both approaches, so you will have a choice. You must be able to make informed, appropriate decisions for any given circumstance. Any way you choose to approach performance, the secret is that you must have the technique and taste to pull it off. Don't allow yourself to be at the mercy of a lack of control of your instrument or lack of knowledge about the form and content of the music.

Each song is an experience, and as life is constantly moving and changing, the possibilities available to you for experiencing the song are vast. There are a few things to consider as you approach a piece.

Technically you must consider the following:

- **Form:** *The order in which the sections of the song are presented*
- **Melody**
- **Rhythm**
- **Lyrics**
- **Range**
- **Harmony**
- **Dynamics:** *written into the song or suggested by the melody or lyrics*

Then you have the emotional content of the song. This is much more problematic, since the technical aspects are concrete and already laid out for you. The emotional content of a song is an intangible. While many singers may master the technical aspects of a song, the "feeling" may still elude them. Conversely, some singers have an innate ability to get to the emotional heart of a song and deliver it with great feeling, while being almost oblivious to the technical aspects of the piece. Our goal as singers should be to combine both.

Have you ever heard a singer who had a beautiful voice but somehow just didn't move you? Or a singer whose instrument was less than stellar, but who sang with such feeling they made you weep? The difference is the way in which they deliver the lyric. A beautiful note reading of the music is not enough to transport a listener unless there is a personal relationship between the singer and the song. *Words are merely empty vessels; you fill them with meaning.* Music is not just a group of notes and words strung together. They must communicate something.

The Zen of Singing ©

The 3 "C's" of Good Performance:

- **Content:** This includes all of the technical aspects of the song, including melody, rhythm, form, and vocal technique.

- **Commitment:** This is the emotional content of the song. Making it real.

- **Creativity:** This includes stylistic and arrangement choices.

Content ~ Commitment ~ Creativity

The first step in performance is choosing and learning a song, the *entire* song, all of the melody notes, words, and different sections *(not just the bridge or first verse...)*. You must know your key and what your arrangement will be. You also need to know how and when you will breathe and use your placement. This is all a part of the <u>Content</u>.

Once you have ALL of the technical parts of a song put together you need to focus on the Point of View *(POV)* of the narrator *(you)*. <u>Commitment</u> requires that you make performance choices about the emotional perspective of the song. Once you have decided what the feeling is, you need to commit to it fully. This is the acting aspect of performance, and it makes the difference between a moving delivery and a stiff, wooden one.

The way in which you make a song yours is the <u>Creativity</u> part of this equation. This could include improvisation, scatting, creating a medley, using unusual instruments or rhythms, most anything you can think of. How you phrase and the feel and arrangements you choose all reflect your choices as a creative artist. Please don't aim to do a note for note rendition of someone else's version of a song. It may be an acceptable way to study at first, but once you are ready to perform it's important to discover what the song says to YOU and share <u>your</u> vision with the listener.

Emotional / Lyrical Content

These are a few things to consider as you are developing your approach to a song.

What is the song about?

You must understand the story if you are to tell it effectively. What is the plot? What exactly is happening, or has happened, in the story?

The Zen of Singing ©

What is the emotional shape of the song?

What is the overriding emotional tone of the song? Is it a song about joy, loss, or love? What kind? How intense is the emotion? Does the emotion change during the course of the song? Does it start quietly and end with a big finish? Does it hit an emotional peak at the *bridge* or *chorus*? Does it move in and out of different levels of intensity? The more specific you can be, the better your chances of capturing the feelings in performance.

What is the " Point Of View" (POV) of the character?

Who are you in the plot? Are you singing about something that happened to your character or something that might happen? Does your *POV* change during the course of the song?

What are you trying to communicate, to whom, and why?

This is MOST important. You must know what you are trying to say with the song, to whom you are directing the information, and why. Are you singing to a lover, a friend, yourself, or a parent? Imagine that person in your head. What may have just happened to make you want to communicate this information to them? Did this friend betray you, or did a lover declare love for you? Perhaps you miss a friend or family member.

Know to WHOM you are singing, and what kind of a response you are trying to get from them. Do you want them to hug you, or feel guilty, or run from you? Create them as an imaginary acting partner and then sing to them in a way that will elicit the response you want from them. See them in your minds eye and SING TO THEM!

Imagine what may have just happened that would have resulted in you singing this song. Write a pre-song script in your head, *in detail*, and use it as motivation for the song.

Go as crazy as you want with the ideas; you can always rein them back in later, and nobody but you needs to know what you are thinking. *(Note: I'm singing "to the audience" is not a strong choice unless it happens to be an audience participation song.)*

Where are you?

Are you in a public place? Alone? Outside? Inside? Warm? Cold? Each possibility can bring something different to the song.

How do you relate to the song?

Sometimes you are assigned songs to sing that you may not feel a real connection to. If this is the case, part of your job is to find a way to relate to the song. Maybe you haven't had the exact experience you are singing about, but if you distill the emotional concept, you will probably find something in your life you can use as a basis from which to develop the character. If the song is about a lover who leaves you for your best friend, even if that never happened to you, it is a song about loss and betrayal, and I'll bet somewhere along the line you have experienced loss or felt betrayed. Connect with those feelings and use them in your delivery.

Think of the lyrics in complete sentences. Each song is a little play. Make sense of the story. Find the plot line. If you have trouble, make use of some actor's tricks: Substitute different emotions, do a Character Study, get specific about where you are *(taste-touch-hear-see-smell)*, who you are *(past, present, future)*, and why you would be singing this song *(what just happened?)* Make strong choices. Vague or overly general choices can result in weak delivery. Don't always play it safe, experiment and stretch a bit. Once you find a focus COMMIT to it!

Those are just a few possible avenues to explore as you prepare a song. Songs are not just random notes and words strung together. Learn to mine the emotional possibilities of each piece and allow them to inform your performance. Bring yourself to each song and understand your material. Remember, singing is communicating. To do it effectively you must have a clear idea of what it is you wish to communicate.   Let   the   song   speak   through   you.

Tips

- Show your inner emotions

- Create imaginary acting partners *(active or passive)*. Make them as real as possible.

- Use subtext/intention to keep P.O.V. *(Point Of View)* interesting.

- Make interesting character choices. One dimensional characters or emotions have no depth or truth.

- Use visualization, inner images, or inner words during "*air*" space between phrases or sections of the song to help you maintain your intensity. Don't be thinking about other things.

Exercises

1.) <u>Role Play:</u> Imitate someone else. Pretend you are Frank Sinatra, Ella Fitzgerald, Bono, Whitney Houston, or any of your favorite singers who has a style that you are very familiar with. While you probably won't sound exactly like them, you will be surprised at how your voice responds and at the control you have. Also, try pretending you are an obvious character. Approach a phrase as if you were an opera singer, surfer, or a wrestler.

2.) Write the lyrics on a separate piece of paper. Read them as you would a story.
a.) Outline the sequence of events in the song
b.) Write the plot line of the story in your own words

3.) Do a Character Study.
Write out: Who, What, When, Where, Why. *(Also refer to the list under Emotional Content.)*

4.) Experiment with changing the emotion. For example, if your first impression of a song is that it is sad, try playing it angry or happy. You don't have to stick with the new emotion, unless it works for you, but you may learn something new about the song from the different perspective.

5.) Why did you choose this song? If you find yourself strongly drawn to a song, spend some time examining why. It may be obvious, or it may take some thought, but it often tells us something about ourselves. Use your journal.

Notes

_____

_____

_____

_____

_____

_____

_____

_____

_____

_____

_____

_____

Don't Fear

Your Fool...

The Zen of Singing ©

11. Performance Anxiety

Don't panic...Have fun!

Performance causes some amount of stress in most people. It would be unnatural if it didn't, but with time and experience it usually abates. A little anxiety can, in fact, help by adding energy to the show, but when it gets in the way of your ability to function effectively you need to learn some tools to help you cope with it. There are examples of famous singers who never got over their stage fright, Barbara Streisand and Ella Fitzgerald to name just two, but they still had wonderful careers. It is part of the journey, and you must learn to deal with it.

There are several things you can do to help with this anxiety. The first line of defense is to **PREPARE ADEQUATELY**! As simple as this sounds, preparation is the most important thing you can do to gain confidence. Know the song upside down and inside out:

1. The arrangement
2. All the words
3. All the correct notes
4. Be clear on your emotional *POV. (See Chapter 10, the Art & Craft of Singing.)*

Learn to be aware of what your body is telling you. Do you feel panic, shortness of breath, dry mouth, fluttering heart, "butterflies", or tense muscles? Most importantly, notice what that little voice in your head is screaming at you: "Oh God, why am I here? I can't sing, they will hate me, everybody will laugh, I'm gonna blow it ", etc. This is where you must learn to focus and calm yourself.

There are as many ways of centering and calming as there are singers: breathing, stretching, meditation, prayer, visualization, chanting, etc. The first thing you have to do is stop that negative self-talk! Find something that works for you. Create a brief calming ritual and use it to pull yourself to your center. If possible, spend some time alone before you go on. Other people can be a major distraction, and it is virtually impossible to command the stage if you are scattered and panicky.

Fear can keep you a prisoner and not allow you to access all the good things you have to bring to your performance, so try to assess clearly what is causing it. We will assume that you are prepared, so here are some general tips that may be useful to you:

Physical issues

New venue? New accompanist? New crowd? The way you look? The way you feel? Is there something new in the space that is making you uncomfortable? Sound, lights, physical space?

Once you can identify the problem, the next step is to relax and adapt to the situation. Accept it, don't fight it. Resisting won't fix the problem and will make you even more uncomfortable.

Emotional issues

Fear of failure, of being judged, of being ridiculed, of feeling inadequate?

These are tricky issues with some people. They often go back to childhood. Perhaps someone told you couldn't sing or laughed at you when you tried to. Maybe you saw someone else embarrassed in performance. There can be even

The Zen of Singing ©

more complex problems that are tied into long-term attitudes about self-worth, etc. Whatever the source, spend some time trying to discover where the fear is coming from and address it.

Concentrate on your strengths, Not your weaknesses.

Try to relax into the experience, and have fun with it. Don't focus on yourself. Focus on your imaginary acting partner. Don't sing *about* a feeling. Sing *from* the feeling. If you are really involved in living the song you won't be able to worry about all that other noise in your head!

If the worst case happens and the performance goes badly, remember that your life will not end. In fact, it can make you a better performer. Learning to deal with the inevitable problems is part of the job description. The bottom line is to realize that, in spite of all our best efforts, everybody falls down from time to time. It is, after all, a learning process. Understand that you are who you are right now... a work in progress. Relish the successes; learn from the mistakes, and MOVE ON!

Tips

- Put your focus outside of you. Don't be *"Self-Conscious"*.

- Use your energy don't hoard it

- **Take** the stage; use your power to control your space *(even if you're faking it!)*

1.) Make a very specific list of all of your perform-ance related fears. *(For example- I am afraid I will forget the words.)* Once you have listed every one you can think of, go back and consider each one. How realistic is it? If it seems reasonable, figure out a solution to the problem, *(If you think you may forget the words practice them more, or under-stand the plot so well that you can improvise, or????)* if it just seems to be overwhelming, try journaling about the source of your fear.

2.) Make a list of how performance fears affect you. Does it manifest physically *(shaky knees or dry mouth)*, or mentally *(brain running 1000 miles an hour, or going blank)* or both?? Again, look for ways to cope with the problems. Suck on a cough drop for dry mouth or meditate before you go on, etc.

The Zen of Singing ©

Discovering Your Diva

Learning to sing well is all fine and good, but how does one go about becoming a *Performer*? Great performers fill the stage with their presence. How does one get the confidence to do that? Well, I believe that deep down inside each of us lives a Diva waiting to be discovered and freed! Where is yours? To answer that question let's get clear on a few things.

First, what kind of performer do you want to be? Spend some time seriously thinking about this. What kind of gigs would you like to do? Small and intimate nightclubs, Broadway, or stadium concerts? Local clubs or Lincoln Center? What kind of music do you really enjoy performing? Does it lend itself to the venues you have in mind? If not, which will you adjust, the music or the choice of venues? Do you see yourself in formal attire or jeans onstage? Conservative or wacky? Go ahead; be bold!

What if this is all too overwhelming and you just can't imagine yourself on stage? Well then, who do you admire on stage? What are they like? Sexy and subtle? Powerful and energetic? Calm and thoughtful? Some combination of all of the above? How do they move and speak? Use the Role Play Exercise *(pg. 86)* and play at being that person. Walk around the room moving and talking like them. Have fun with this, don't get too serious. Give yourself permission to PLAY at it! You probably won't move or sound exactly like the character you are modeling, but you should notice how much it changes the way you normally walk and talk.

Once you feel comfortable playing, try singing as this character. See how much fun it can be if you just relax and allow yourself to be silly? Having fun is very freeing and powerful. Audiences love to watch people having fun. Think of it from their perspective. Would you want to go watch a performer who was obviously uptight or terrified? I think not. But, if you are enjoying yourself it shows and is appreciated by audiences. If _you_ are having fun, they are more likely to have fun and to be forgiving of any mistakes that might happen.

Yes, mistakes will happen, for everyone. More than once! Even the highest end pros make mistakes. The difference is that they don't let the mistakes stop them. *(Or define them...)* Accept, recover, and move on, instantly and graciously. Smile kiddo, it's just a goof.

Clarify your "Diva" vision and allow it to take up residence as your stage personality, your performance alter ego. Believe me, most of us have way too much baggage to take the stage as our everyday selves, so create yourself a fearless stage persona and let them do it for you. It's very freeing!

The Zen of Singing ©

Meet Your Diva

Visualization 2
(on the CD)

Sit or lie comfortably and relax. Count your breaths and clear your mind. As you relax, allow your mind to call up your ideal performance situation. Go into great detail and really try to see, hear, and feel it. Listen to the musicians tuning up and preparing for your entrance. The seats are all filled, and there is great anticipation and excitement in the room because the audience is looking forward to your performance. What does the stage look like? Is it a small cabaret size theatre or a huge concert hall? A small coffeehouse stage, or a giant amphitheatre? What is the lighting like? Orchestra, band or solo piano accompanist? See, hear and feel it all.

See yourself waiting in the wings for your entrance. What are you wearing? How do you feel? You hear your name announced and the crowd cheering for your entrance. See yourself walking out onto the stage and acknowledging the applause and devotion of the crowd. How are you moving and standing? With grace and confidence? How is your presence occupying the stage? What song will you sing? See yourself singing it superbly. The crowd cheers wildly as you take your bow and exit, only to return as the crowd calls out for more. Bask in the success of your performance!

Sometimes, our first shot at this exercise is less than a rousing success. We may see ourselves stumble or make a mistake during the scene. Not to worry! This is a movie that we write, direct, and act out in our heads, so we just keep redoing the scene until we get it exactly as we want it. Each time thru the exercise it gets easier and more detailed. Once you have it just the way you want it, replay it often. Change it whenever you want. The "Diva" you created then becomes your performance model. Allow your Diva to take the stage.

<u>Journal about the following:</u>

- Explore the details. What you saw, what you heard, what you felt.

- Any surprises?

- Did anything change as you went along?

- Did the scene go as you had hoped or planned? Why?

- Could you allow yourself to enjoy the scene as it unfolded, or were you resistant to it? *(I don't deserve this, I'll never get this, etc...)*

- Does the scene evolve as you repeat it? How?

Notes

_____

_____

_____

_____

_____

_____

_____

_____

_____

_____

_____

_____

_____

Lay the Foundation

And Clear the Path

For your Muse...

12. Singers as Musicians

Understanding "Form" is key to finding your creative voice.

Basics

If you want to be taken seriously as a singer, you need to have a rudimentary understanding of music theory. Music is a language, and you must become conversant in the basics. If you don't know anything about *key signatures, time signatures, measures, form,* standard *intros* and *tags,* or *feel,* communication on the bandstand becomes virtually impossible.

The simplest ideas can become train wrecks if communication breaks down. Singers with a wonderful natural talent and a terrific "ear" must still know how to explain their needs to a band. Even great musicians who want to support you are at a disadvantage if you can't tell them what you need. Nothing sours a band's attitude towards a singer more quickly than, " I don't know about keys... I just sing it here." *(Followed by a warbled note...)*

If you expect real musicians to be willing to work with you, you need to respect them, and yourself, enough to prepare and behave like a professional. At the very least, know your keys, tempos, style/feel of a tune, and be able to explain your arrangement, even if you have the chart or sheet music. If you do have the music, make sure it is in the right key and that you perform it as written or can communicate whatever the differences are.

Not being able to do this is inexcusable. If you know nothing at all about music, you can begin by learning the above information by rote for each song. Have a musician friend help you with it. For each of your songs you need:

- **Song Title**

- **Your Key:** The key determines your starting note.

- **Feel/Style**: Funk, Bossa Nova, Swing, Ballad, Blues, Hip-Hop, etc.

- **Tempo:** How fast or slow you want it

- **Arrangement Notes:** Introduction & Ending or anything special.

Write it down, memorize it, and be able to recite it. Meanwhile, get educated! The information is readily available, so take classes or private lessons, get a book or video, go online ... No excuses. This is part of learning your craft, so DO it! Please, for all of our sakes, avoid the bands eyes rolling back in their heads because another "bimbo" singer *(this goes for you guys, too...)* has taken the stage. When you get on the stage, make it yours because you are sure of yourself, where you are going, what you need to get there, and HOW TO GET IT!

If you are naturally very musical you may get by fairly well with little or no theory. After all, the music came before the written explanation of it, *(written theory is only about 400 years old)* and good ears will take you a long way. Still, as you progress, the more understanding you have of the basics, the more easily you will be able to deal with the demands of being a performer.

The Zen of Singing ©

Warning... Here Comes a Rant:

I am amazed when singers think they can get by with no under-standing of basic music theory. It leaves them virtually helpless to create their own sound or arrangement, not to mention mak-ing them a HUGE pain for the band. With an understanding of just a FEW of the basics you can be the captain of your own ship.

In a perfect world you should have some facility on an instru-ment, but even if you don't, the good news is that you don't need to become a master sight-reader *(although it wouldn't hurt and could open up a career as a studio musician)*, but learning a few basics about keys, feel, form and how to put together a chart will make a major difference. O.K., end of rant... Phew!

Tips

- ALWAYS know where "ONE" is. *(The first beat of the measure)*

- "Good Time" is imperative. So is a good sense of the "Tonal Center." Know where you fit into the sonic picture.

- Know what keys you do your songs in. The difference between singing a song in F or Bb could make or break you in a tune. Find a key that suits you. *(In spite of what the band may say, there is no "right" key, but do them a favor and avoid keys with too many sharps or flats)*

- Singers in bands: Listen to the Bass. The bass usually anchors a song to its key.

- Also listen to what the band is doing, not just your own notes. How do they fit together? Music is a WHOLE thing, made up of several parts. How does your part fit in to make it work as a whole?

- Learn to play an instrument. It really helps put things in perspective.

Have "BIG EARS" ~ listen...listen...listen!

The Zen of Singing ©

Exercises

1. Work with recorded tracks and practice finding your entrance and various sections of the song.

2. Tape Drills: Record songs with various intros & styles.

3. Groove Drill: Try the same song at different tempos and with different feels. A drum machine is a handy practice tool.

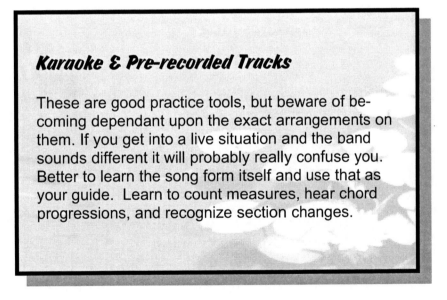

Karaoke & Pre-recorded Tracks

These are good practice tools, but beware of becoming dependant upon the exact arrangements on them. If you get into a live situation and the band sounds different it will probably really confuse you. Better to learn the song form itself and use that as your guide. Learn to count measures, hear chord progressions, and recognize section changes.

Form

Simply put, *"Form"* is the order the various sections of the song are in. Each section of the song is made up of a certain number of measures, usually 8 or 16. This is especially true of songs that follow the traditional 32 bar form *(exclusive of intro, verse or ending)*. More contemporary music can differ from this standard form.

We often call the Verses **"A** Sections" and the Chorus the **"B** Section". There can also be C or even D sections. A standard form might be Verse, Verse, Chorus, Verse, which is **A A B A**.

Tips

- The *form* is determined by the melody of the song. Sing it in your head during solos.

- Standard pop forms include: AABA, AAA, ABAB, ABCA

- Always know where you are in the song - even when others are soloing.

- Learn to feel the different sections of a song.

- Listen for Harmonic or Chord Progression clues.

The Zen of Singing ©

Notes

_____

_____

_____

_____

_____

_____

_____

_____

_____

_____

_____

_____

Color Outside

The Lines,

Fearlessly...

The Zen of Singing ©

13. Improvisation

Style develops with experience.

Improvisation is used in many styles of music from Rock, to Country, to Reggae, to many forms of World Music, and of course Jazz and Blues. *(It even used to be common in Classical Music... in fact Mozart was, by all accounts, a great improviser)* I work in the Jazz arena, so that is the context I will use for discussion, but the ideas work across the board.

The word "jazz" was used to describe a particular form of music called "swing", but over the years it has come to describe a number of different styles of music built around the concept of improvisation. I consider jazz an approach to music, based on improvisation. There are "Song Stylists" who have jazz-like phrasing but have memorized the lines and sing it exactly the same way each time. Some of them are quite good singers, and there is nothing wrong with what they do, but the bottom line is; if there's no improvisation it's not jazz, no matter what the style is. Improvisation is not limited to *scat singing*. It begins with the way you approach a phrase, allowing a song to inform you and having the craft to let it speak. We will get further into that later, but first a word about how music happens.

Have you ever wondered how musicians who have never met can get on stage together and make such great music? It is because they share a common language and understanding of music, form, and harmony. Improvising doesn't mean getting up and playing with no rules or concept. There is an entire body of music, often called *"Standards"*, that any player worth his salt has a working knowledge of. So, when they play a tune they agree on the key, tempo, feel, and form, *(just like you are expected to do)* and then they have the freedom to experiment with the possibilities inherent in that structure. If they decide to go outside those boundaries they must communicate their intent to everyone else. While occasionally instrumentals have such loose structures that they may appear to have no rules, the players must still come to some kind of agreement about the journey they are about to take together.

Singers are, for the most part, given a form within which to work. It is <u>the song</u>. It tells you the structure *(form)*, which is based on the melody. Harmony adds interest, but the melody really defines the parameters of the song. The first thing you need to do is to figure out the form of the song. Is it a standard form or not? Once that is understood you have a good handle for always knowing where you are in a song. In most cases the form is just repeated over and over. *(The exception being if there is an "arrangement", which informs every one of the variations)*

If you always find yourself lost during the band's solos, try singing the melody in your head while they are playing, that should keep you locked into the form. It might be confusing at first, but it will soon make sense. With practice it can become second nature and will make your life MUCH easier.

Tips

- Internalize the melody and the beat. Feel it!

- Be very clear on the form.

- Listen... don't think too much

The Zen of Singing ©

Phrasing

Improvisation isn't limited to scatting or instrumental solos. Good singers are constantly improvising with the melody and the way they approach a phrase. A stiff note reading gets boring very quickly. Remember, a song is not merely a group of notes and words, or syllables and pitches. Learn to think of the phrases as complete thoughts, and don't merely sing from note to note. Make sense of what you are singing, and natural phrasing will easily follow.

Once you have a clear idea of what you are saying, the melody provides a wealth of possibilities. *(See Emotional Content, pg.82)* You can play with the phrase rhythmically, melodically, dynamically, or with tone color. The lyric and mood of the song should suggest any number of options.

Music is made up of sound **and** silence. The silence gives the sound weight. Without it the sound would soon become monotonous. Besides the silence written into the song itself, as rests, you have the option of including it in the way you phrase. Well-placed silence adds depth to lyrics. For example read the following phrase out loud and leave a very brief pause where you see the dots:

I LOVE YOU *(no pause)*   I....... LOVE YOU

I LOVE ....YOU   I.... LOVE ..... YOU

The words remain the same, but the silence changed the feeling a bit. We normally use this *"space"* or *"air"* when we speak to each other. We don't run words together without pause, we use space to emphasize and focus attention. Popular music often has a very natural speech-like cadence. Listen to the great singers and notice how they use it too.

You also have choices as to how you use dynamics and even how you play around with the melody. Adding a riff or changing the melody a bit here and there can also add interest and emotional impact. Just be sure it sounds natural and not forced. Don't go overboard with it, keep the integrity of the song intact.

While it's always good to study other singers, also listen to how instrumentalists phrase. Don't get stuck in a habit because you heard another singer phrase it this way or that way. Open your ears to all the possibilities. Don't copy anyone else's version or arrangement of a song. <u>Experiment!</u>

Tips

- Phrase from the intention of the lyric, but give way if it doesn't make musical sense.

- Breathe when you need it. It's not a contest to see how long a phrase you can sing.

- Carrying a note " over the bar" can help fill up the "*air*" space, but don't overdo it.

- A song is divided into time units called "measures". Each measure is then sub-divided into equal parts. The sound or accents, which occur on the sub-divided beats, creates a "rhythm" pattern. Learn to subdivide a 4/4 measure into 12/8 to help break up the rhythm *(Example on CD)*

The Zen of Singing ©

Notes

Five Ways to be Creative Within a Song

(CD Examples)

1. **Melody:** Simple variations and articulations of pitches including:

   Slides: *Sliding up or down between notes*
   Changes: *Varying the melody*

   Decorations: *Adding notes or melodic phrases called "Riffs"*

2. **Rhythm:** Duration of the notes . Breaking the rhythm up in different ways, using more or less *"air" (space between notes)*. Also, delaying or singing just behind the beat, *(Back- phrasing)*, just ahead of it, or right "on top" of it.

3. **Phrasing:** Smooth *(Legato)* or choppy *(Staccato)*

4. **Dynamics:** Volume, intensity

5. **Color/Texture:** Type of tone: pure, breathy, rich, thin, warm, edgy, growl, whine, etc.

The Zen of Singing ©

Arrangements

Another great tool for creating your own version of a song is an arrangement. Don't do a rehash of someone else's version. Make the song your own!

Possibilities for Arrangements

1. **Tempo:** How fast or slow the song is

2. **Feel:** Style choice (Ballad, Samba, Funk, Hip-Hop, etc)

3. **Form:** You can extend, add, repeat or shorten, create Medleys, and choose Intros & Endings

Scat Singing
(Examples on CD)

Scatting is singing a melodic line using syllables instead of words. It is an improvisational avenue that is open to singers. It can be more freeing than sticking with a lyric, it can also be VERY challenging. You need good ears, a quick mind, and a very coordinated instrument.

Start by listening to great scat singers. *(Ella Fitzgerald, Jon Hendricks, Leo Watson, Al Jarreau, etc.)* Listen to how they are working with the form. Once you are clear on what they are doing, and how it relates to what is going on in the music, try "*copping*" a few of their "*licks*". *(Singing a few of their lines.)* Build yourself a vocabulary of "licks" and start combining them in different ways. Also, listen to instrumental solos. Eventually these should suggest new ideas, and you will discover your own territory.

Remember, what you sing must be related to what is happening harmonically and rhythmically in the song, so listen...listen.... listen! Listening, by the way, is one of the foremost skills required of a good singer.

Once you have a few simple licks under your belt, begin to play with them. Start with a simple one bar melodic motif, or riff. Then begin to build your scat ideas by:

       1.) **Repeating** the riff

       2.) **Changing** the riff *(Rhythm or melody notes)*

       3.) **Adding** to the riff *(New syllables or melodic embellishments)*

       4.) **Resolving** an idea *(Answering or finishing the thought)*

The Zen of Singing ©

Play with the original riff and find as many different possibilities as you can and see where the ideas lead you. Then work ideas within the context of a song.

Beginners: Stay close to the melody and keep it simple.

Advanced: Explore possibilities that are further from the melody. Play with scales and chords to stretch your harmonic ideas.

Tips

- Internalize the beat. *(Feel the pulse in your body)*

- Use short musical ideas or phrases *(Motifs)*

- Phrases should build tension and release it.

Conclusion

After rereading what I have written I realize that I have barely scratched the surface of the subject of singing. After a lifetime of study and thought I am still learning things on a daily basis. I will never know it all *(thankfully)* and neither will anyone else. My goal is to continue the journey and celebrate the joy that music and teaching bring to my life.

I hope that these few thoughts I have put together have been of interest and use to you. Your path won't and shouldn't look like anyone else's. My hope for you is that you can discover the joy in the journey itself and that you are able to integrate singing into your life in a way that makes <u>you</u> happy.

Be fearless,

Have fun, and...

Fly, Be Free!

The Zen of Singing ©

Appendix

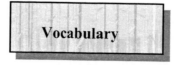

Vocabulary

Air: The silence or "space" between notes.

Back Phrasing: Melody note is sung after the accompanying *chord* or just behind the beat

Blowing: Playing your instrument- singing

Chord: A group of notes sounded simultaneously

Chord Progression: A series of chords played in succession.

Coda: ⊕ A sign that indicates where the ending is *(Also see **Tag**)*

Copping: Borrowing or stealing someone else's ideas

Crescendo: Becoming gradually louder.

Decrescendo: becoming gradually softer.

Dynamics: How loudly or softly you sing

Face Masque: The area in the front of your face above the roof of your mouth.

Feel: Style of the music. *(E.g.: Bossa Nova, Swing, etc...)*

Flat: *(b)* A sign that tells you to play the named note ½ step lower

Form: The order the sections of the song are in

Gigs: Musical jobs, performances

Harmonic: Relating to the harmony of a song.

Head: Where the melody of the song begins

Interval: The sonic distance between notes.

The Zen of Singing ©

Intro: How you begin the song: Usually added *measures*, sometimes a single note, or *chord*. It introduces your *tonal center* and *feel*.

Key Signature: Determines your starting note. It tells you how many sharps or flats are in the scale used

Legato: Smooth and flowing

Licks: Short melodic ideas (*also called Riffs*)

Melodic: relating to the melody of a song.

Messa de Voce: Gradually getting louder, then softer.

Motif: A short melodic phrase

Riffs: See *Licks*

Scale Degrees: The numbering system assigned to the notes of a scale.

Scatting: Singing a melody using syllables rather than words.

Sharp:(#) A sign that tells you to play the named note ½ step higher (e.g. F becomes F#)

Staccato: Quick or choppy

Standards: Familiar songs that are part of the common experience of most professionals

Style: See *Feel*

Tag: How you end the song. (*Also the Outro or Coda*)

Tempo: How fast or slow a song is going.

Tessitura: Where the basic range of a melody or voice lies, not including the occasional high or low note.

Tonal Center: The appropriate relationship of the notes to the key *(Knowing where the **tonic** of the key or chord is)*

Tonic: The **1** or starting note of a *key* or *chord.*

Triad: A 3-note chord. The quality may be Major, Minor, Diminished or Augmented.

Vocalese: 1) Writing/ singing lyrics to a famous instrumental solo **2)** Improvisation using words instead of scatting. Often, but not always, created on the spot. *(Or developed over time from an on- the- spot improvisation.)*

The Zen of Singing ©

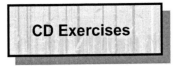

CD Exercises

The exercises should be done <u>gently</u>, consistently, and most of all *mindfully*. They are simple enough that you should be able to truly PAY ATTENTION to what you are doing. The CD begins with "Long Tones". Single notes that you hold to get focused on the sound. The single notes are the building blocks, so we need to make sure they are solid. They are also the least complicated exercises, so you can really concentrate on hearing and feeling everything that is going on. This is a good exercise on which to use "The Scan". *(Pg. 18)*

Next comes a little interval work. Intervals will help train your ear. Make sure you are very precise as you work them; don't slide around or use sloppy tone. Once you feel comfortable with them, move on to the other exercises. Take them slowly and don't overwhelm yourself at first. One or two exercises per session are fine to start with.

Now the bad news: This is not magic... you have to practice if you want to improve. Intending to practice is nice, but all the intention in the world is no good if you don't do the work! If you are serious about singing, you need to do serious practicing. If you are just in it for some fun, you can be a bit less disciplined. Remember, 5 minutes here and there is better than zero minutes, but you will improve in direct proportion to the amount of work you invest. You get from it what you give to it....

Have fun, don't worry, and make it joyful!

The CD

Guided Visualizations:

Experience Your Breath *(pg 39)*
Meet Your Diva *(pg 97)*

Examples

Sub-dividing Measures *(Pg.112)*
5 Ways to Be Creative *(Pg. 114)*
Scatting Example *(Pg.116)*

Warm Up

Start your warm up by sighing. A nice relaxed "AAAAAhhh..."

Long-Tones

I play the note 3 times. Sing each repetition individually and/ or hold the note as long as is comfortable through the series of 3. For those of you who have trouble matching pitches, use them to learn to focus your ear: 1st time - *Listen,* 2nd time - *Clarify,* and 3rd time - *Sing.* Focus and be precise

Intervals:

I have included very basic interval work based on Scale Degrees *(Pg.127)*. The 1-3-5-8 intervals are fundamental and will help you to sing in tune as well as train your ear.

Vocal Exercises:

Once you are comfortable with the long-tones and intervals move on to exercises number 1- 7. They are simple scales and arpeggios. Once you have mastered them, the Alternative Exercises may be substituted for the same numbered exercises. Be sure not to sing higher or lower than is comfortable. Never push or strain!

The Zen of Singing ©

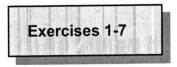

1.) Bubbling Lips

This does not take much air. It requires control and focus. More sound... less air.

2.) "Where Shall I Go Today" or Rolling "R"s your choice.

If you have trouble with rolling "R's, try starting with a "TH" sound. Just flip it off your tongue. It should be relaxed, NOT tense. *ALTERNATE:* 1-3-5-8-5-3-1 *(Scale Degree Intervals)*

3.) AH ..... AYE......EE.....OH.......OO......

Aim for consistency in the sound from note to note
ALTERNATE: EE- OO   EE-OO EE-OO or Nyow

4.) AH, AYE,EE,OH,OO....OO

One breath please, smooth and consistent sound.

5.) Ni ... Ni.... Ni...Ni....Ni

Use the "N" to get the sound high in the face masque
ALTERNATE: 1-3-5-3-1 *(Scale Degree Intervals)*

6.) Ma May Mi Mow Moo

You may also " Na, Nay, etc..

7.) Octave Long Tones

Again aim for consistent tone. Use vibrato only at the end of the tone.

1.) Sing on vowel sounds and diphthongs
(e.g.: Meow, Night, Now...) Legato *(Sustained breath control and support)*

2.) "Ha ... Ha... Ha...": Staccato *(Use your diaphragm! Squeeze on attack and release between each note.)*

3.) Ka...Kay... Ki... Ko ... Koo:
Try to keep the attack out of the throat. *(Vary the consonant e.g.: Ta, Fa, Da etc...)*

4.) Hilly Lilly ... O *(Milly, Tilly, Silly, Billy, Filly Lilly ... Also, try inserting the articulation phrases)*

5.) NYA , Nya Nya Nya Nya

6.) La Lay Li Low Loo *(Vary the consonant)*

7.) Octave Crescendo & Decrescendo: Smoothly, don't start too loudly, or you will have no place to go. Support!

The Zen of Singing ©

What are Scale Degrees?

The standard major scale (*do re mi fa so la ti do*) is made up of 8 notes. So, 1-3-5 would be the 1st, 3rd and 5th notes of the scale, no matter what the key signature.

Key of C Major

Note Names:	C	D	E	F	G	A	B	C
Scale Degrees:	1	2	3	4	5	6	7	8
Solfeggio:	do	re	mi	fa	sol	la	ti	do

*So, if you sing **1-3-5-8** in C Major you are singing:*
C-E-G-C** or **do- mi- sol- do

More advanced:

The type, or quality, of the Triads *(3 note chords)* built upon the scale degrees are noted below using Roman Numerals. Upper case is a Major Triad, Lower case is a Minor Triad and the tiny "0" on the 7th degree denotes a Diminished Triad.

Chord Quality:

I   ii   iii   IV   V   vi   vii^{o} VIII

Understanding these concepts will help A LOT!!

The more you listen to, read and think about music, the more your instrument will respond!

Further Reading:

There are many, many singing books on the market today, covering a wide range of topics and perspectives. I encourage you to explore as many of them as possible. Learning is a lifetime process. Here are just a few of my favorites:

Effortless Mastery by Kenny Werner (_Pub: Jamey Abersold Jazz_)
A great guide to the transcendent experience of music. w/CD

The Clippinger Class Method by D.A. Clippinger (_Pub: Oliver Ditson)_
Though written in 1932, this vocal technique book is still a standard.

Tipbook: Vocal by Hugo Pinksterboer (_Pub: The tipbook Company)_
Concise and handy. Also has weblinks for more info.

Vocal Improvistaion by Michelle Weir (_Pub: Advance Music)_
A very thorough exploration of vocal improvisation technique. w/CD

Complete Singers Guide by Wayland Pickard _(Pub: Pickard Publishing_
Packed with info about the nuts & bolts of being a working singer.

Musicianship for Singers by Jeffrey Deutsch (_Pub: Hal Leonard)_
Music theory is a must for serious singers. w/CD

The Complete Idiots Guide to Music Theory by Michael Miller (_Pub: Penguin)_ Hate the title, love the info. Easy to use and understand.

Blues Scatitudes by Bob Stoloff (_Pub: Gerard & Sarzin)_
Learn to scat over the blues. w/CD

**That's just to start with, there are MANY, MANY more!**

Also note that **Jamey Abersold** has an entire catalogue of great titles that are useful to singers. They cover theory as well as many sing-along tracks. Look for them online at : **www.abersold.com**

Thanks:

Thanks to all of my students through the years who have taught me so much, to the teachers who have coped with me, and to my friends who have supported me. Thank you to Cherie Kerr, a wonderful teacher and dear friend, who gave me the great gift of allowing me to work with her. Special thanks to Karen Schmedeke for help with the artwork, Hildegarde Gechter, and David Belo, my editor, supporter, and beloved friend.

Credits:

Graphics & Cover Design: Karen Schmedeke

Layout: Karen Gallinger and Dave Belo

Illustrations on pages: 40, 49, 56, 57, 58, : Karen Gallinger

Photos on pages: 47, 59 by Karen Gallinger

Model: Dave Belo

Editor/ Proof Reading & All Around Hero: Dave Belo

CD Recorded at: Lynda Roth Studios

Recording Engineer: Lynda Roth

Please contact Ms. Gallinger if you have questions, comments, problems with the CD or wish to give us feedback on our products. Online (*ZenofSinging.com*) or by mail at :

P.O. Box 204 ~ East Irvine ~ CA ~ USA ~ 92650-0204

The Zen of Singing ©

Contact:

P.O. Box 204 ~ East Irvine
CA ~ USA ~ 92650-0204

www.Jazzgal.com

About the Author:

The L.A. Weekly calls Karen Gallinger *"A voice of extraordinary range and quality."* With 4 CD's in international distribution, she is also an educator, composer, lyricist, writer, and producer. She brings a lifetime of performance experience to this book.

Long regarded one of Southern California's finest jazz vocalists, Karen Gallinger blends artistic passion and mastery of her craft into a dynamic and unique package. As a vocalist, her original sense of humor and *"casual hipness" (Jazz Now)* combine with her interpretive abilities to give her an artistic range that is *"stylish and sultry" (O.C. Register)* as well as *"simply fun and irresistible." (L.A. Weekly)*

A private vocal teacher for over 20 years, Gallinger has done clinics and master classes ranging from technique to performance skills. Besides her busy private coaching, she is on staff at The DePietro Performance Center and The Orange County High School of the Arts, where she teaches voice and theatre.

Also a gifted composer and lyricist, her lyrics to a number of Bill Evans songs have been recorded by singers Tierney Sutton and Roseanna Vitro, among others. Ms. Gallinger appears at concerts, festivals and nightclubs in the USA, Europe and Asia.

When she is not traveling, Ms. Gallinger lives in California.

Recordings by Karen Gallinger

Kinda Blues
MindsEye Jazz, 2004

Remembering Bill Evans - A Vocal Tribute
Sea Breeze Jazz, 2000

My Foolish Heart
Sea Breeze Jazz, 1998

Live At The Jazz Bakery
Sea Breeze Jazz, 1995

**Available at most retail outlets including:
Tower, Borders, Amazon, CD Baby,
and Jazzgal.com**

The Zen of Singing ©

Karen Gallinger

is available for Concerts, Workshops, Seminars, and Master Classes.

Check the website for more Vocal Tips, Classes and Artist Info:

www.ZenofSinging.com

949) 291-1417

or contact the artist directly at

www.Jazzgal.com

To order products directly, please send Check or Money Order to:

Karen Gallinger
P.O. Box 204 ~ East Irvine
CA ~ USA ~ 92650-0204

<u>**Title & Quantity**</u>   <u>**Cost**</u>

Book:

_____ *The Zen of Singing ($18.95 ea)*   _____

CD's: *($15 ea)*

_____ *Live at the Jazz Bakery*   _____

_____ *My Foolish Heart*   _____

_____ *Remembering Bill Evans*   _____

_____ *Kinda Blues*   _____

Add Shipping & Handling ($2.50 per item)   _____

Total: _____

Include your shipping information

Please allow 4-6 weeks for delivery.

The Zen of Singing ©